# Lepanto

# *Lepanto*

## by G. K. Chesterton

With explanatory notes
and commentary

Edited by Dale Ahlquist

IGNATIUS PRESS    SAN FRANCISCO

Cover art from a woodcut by Simon Brett
Cover design by Julian Ahlquist

# CONTENTS

# INTRODUCTION

*Lepanto* is not only one of G. K. Chesterton's finest poems; it is one of the finest poems in the English language. It is an intricate tapestry of images, an evocative telling of history, and a masterpiece of rhyme and rhythm and alliteration.

The Battle of Lepanto was fought on Sunday, October 7, 1571, just south of the town of Lepanto (now Naupaktos), Greece, in the Gulf of Lepanto (Naupaktos), which adjoins the Gulf of Patras on the west and the Gulf of Corinth on the east. The battle was a key turning point in history. The Islamic forces under Selim II controlled the Mediterranean and were threatening to attack both Venice and Rome, which could have led to the collapse of Christian Europe. The poem brings out the fact that the odds are against Christendom in this monumental standoff. The Holy League will get no help from Germany, divided and weakened by the Protestant Reformation; or from England, under the self-absorbed "cold queen", Elizabeth I; or from France, under the worthless "shadow of the Valois", King Charles IX. But a surprise hero rises to the occasion: the "last knight of Europe", twenty-four-year-old Don John of Austria, illegitimate son of Emperor Charles V, who miraculously leads the Christian forces to victory.

Chesterton's poem not only tells the story; it truly stirs the emotions. He takes a very creative approach, describing different perspectives of the events, from the sneering and plotting Sultan in his Eastern courts, to Muhammad strutting in his paradise, to the Pope praying in the Vatican, to the Christian slaves chained to their oars in the Muslim galley ships, and, finally, to a certain Spanish warrior who was wounded in the victory and later went on to become a rather noted author: Cervantes. Marching through each of these scenes, as to the sound of a beating drum, is the heroic Don John of Austria.

For the explanatory notes on the poem, we have tried whenever possible to offer explanations from Chesterton himself, that is, excerpts from his other writings that shed light on his imagery and ideas.

The commentaries are designed to show that one of the reasons the poem is so significant is that the battle itself was so significant. An essay on the historical background of the famous battle was prepared by Brandon Rogers, who succinctly describes the state of western Europe and the Ottoman Empire in the sixteenth century. For an account of the battle itself, we were pleased to be able to call on a true soldier, Col. Buzz Kriesel. Next, the effect that the battle had on the rest of world history, right up to the present day, is discussed by Will Cinfici. These fine essays are followed by a piece of bosh trying to pass itself off as literary criticism, offered by this editor in an attempt to fill up some space.

Finally, we include two essays by G.K. Chesterton that are connected to this topic. One was written just before the poem, and the other long after. His observations on a genuinely romantic character are amusing. But his reflections on Don John and Mary Queen of Scots are amazing. If we were to annotate that essay, explaining all the historical references, it would triple the size of this book. Chesterton not only demonstrates his mastery of history but, more interestingly, of the history that might have been. And the conclusion is especially powerful and provocative.

But the most important piece in this book is Chesterton's great poem. It is our hope that it will be studied and enjoyed by a new generation, and generations to come.

This project was instigated and watched over by Peter Floriani. There is no way to possibly acknowledge our debt to him for all that he has done to make this book possible. We are also grateful to the late F.J. (Jim) Slattery, of the Australian Chesterton Society, who gave us some helpful notes. And thanks, too, to Ian Boyd, C.S.B., who pointed us in the right direction on one particularly mystifying reference.

And our deepest thanks to Simon Brett, who kindly granted us permission to reproduce details from his wonderful woodcuts of *Lepanto*.

Dale Ahlquist
President
American Chesterton Society

*Stiff flags straining in the night-blasts cold . . .*

# *Lepanto*

### G. K. Chesterton

White founts falling in the courts of the sun,
And the Soldan of Byzantium is smiling as they run;
There is laughter like the fountains in that face of all
　　men feared,
It stirs the forest darkness, the darkness of his beard,
5　It curls the blood-red crescent, the crescent of his lips,
For the inmost sea of all the earth is shaken with his
　　ships.
They have dared the white republics up the capes of
　　Italy,
They have dashed the Adriatic round the Lion of the
　　Sea,
And the Pope has cast his arms abroad for agony and
　　loss,
10　And called the kings of Christendom for swords about
　　the Cross,
The cold queen of England is looking in the glass;
The shadow of the Valois is yawning at the Mass;
From evening isles fantastical rings faint the Spanish
　　gun,
And the Lord upon the Golden Horn is laughing in
　　the sun.

15　Dim drums throbbing, in the hills half heard,
Where only on a nameless throne a crownless prince
　　has stirred,

Where, risen from a doubtful seat and half-attainted
    stall,
The last knight of Europe takes weapons from the
    wall,
The last and lingering troubadour to whom the bird
    has sung,
20    That once went singing southward when all the world
    was young,
In that enormous silence, tiny and unafraid,
Comes up along a winding road the noise of the
    Crusade.
Strong gongs groaning as the guns boom far,
Don John of Austria is going to the war,
25    Stiff flags straining in the night-blasts cold
In the gloom black-purple, in the glint old-gold,
Torchlight crimson on the copper kettle-drums,
Then the tuckets, then the trumpets, then the cannon,
    and he comes.
Don John laughing in the brave beard curled,
30    Spurning of his stirrups like the thrones of all the
    world,
Holding his head up for a flag of all the free.
Love-light of Spain—hurrah!
Death-light of Africa!
Don John of Austria
35    Is riding to the sea.

Mahound is in his paradise above the evening star,
(*Don John of Austria is going to the war.*)
He moves a mighty turban on the timeless houri's
    knees,
His turban that is woven of the sunset and the seas.

40 He shakes the peacock gardens as he rises from his
ease,
And he strides among the tree-tops and is taller than
the trees,
And his voice through all the garden is a thunder sent
to bring
Black Azrael and Ariel and Ammon on the wing.
Giants and the Genii,
45 Multiplex of wing and eye,
Whose strong obedience broke the sky
When Solomon was king.

They rush in red and purple from the red clouds of
the morn,
From temples where the yellow gods shut up their
eyes in scorn;
50 They rise in green robes roaring from the green hells
of the sea
Where fallen skies and evil hues and eyeless creatures
be;
On them the sea-valves cluster and the grey sea-forests
curl,
Splashed with a splendid sickness, the sickness of the
pearl;
They swell in sapphire smoke out of the blue cracks
of the ground,—
55 They gather and they wonder and give worship to
Mahound.
And he saith, "Break up the mountains where the
hermit-folk may hide,
And sift the red and silver sands lest bone of saint
abide,
And chase the Giaours flying night and day, not giving
rest,

For that which was our trouble comes again out of
the west.

60 We have set the seal of Solomon on all things under
sun,

Of knowledge and of sorrow and endurance of things
done,

But a noise is in the mountains, in the mountains,
and I know

The voice that shook our palaces—four hundred years
ago:

It is he that saith not 'Kismet'; it is he that knows not
Fate;

65 It is Richard, it is Raymond, it is Godfrey in the gate!

It is he whose loss is laughter when he counts the
wager worth,

Put down your feet upon him, that our peace be on
the earth."

For he heard drums groaning and he heard guns jar,

(*Don John of Austria is going to the war.*)

70 Sudden and still—hurrah!

Bolt from Iberia!

Don John of Austria

Is gone by Alcalar.


St. Michael's on his Mountain in the sea-roads of the
north

75 (*Don John of Austria is girt and going forth.*)

Where the grey seas glitter and the sharp tides shift

And the sea folk labour and the red sails lift.

He shakes his lance of iron and he claps his wings of
stone;

The noise is gone through Normandy; the noise is
gone alone;

80    The North is full of tangled things and texts and ach-
            ing eyes
       And dead is all the innocence of anger and surprise,
       And Christian killeth Christian in a narrow dusty
            room,
       And Christian dreadeth Christ that hath a newer face
            of doom,
       And Christian hateth Mary that God kissed in Galilee,
85    But Don John of Austria is riding to the sea.
       Don John calling through the blast and the eclipse
       Crying with the trumpet, with the trumpet of his
            lips,
       Trumpet that sayeth ha!
       *Domino gloria!*
90    Don John of Austria
       Is shouting to the ships.

       King Philip's in his closet with the Fleece about his
            neck
       (*Don John of Austria is armed upon the deck.*)
       The walls are hung with velvet that is black and soft
            as sin,
95    And little dwarfs creep out of it and little dwarfs creep
            in.
       He holds a crystal phial that has colours like the moon,
       He touches, and it tingles, and he trembles very soon,
       And his face is as a fungus of a leprous white and grey
       Like plants in the high houses that are shuttered from
            the day,
100   And death is in the phial, and the end of noble work,
       But Don John of Austria has fired upon the Turk.
       Don John's hunting, and his hounds have bayed—
       Booms away past Italy the rumour of his raid.
       Gun upon gun, ha! ha!

105    Gun upon gun, hurrah!
       Don John of Austria
       Has loosed the cannonade.


       The Pope was in his chapel before day or battle broke,
       (*Don John of Austria is hidden in the smoke.*)
110    The hidden room in a man's house where God sits all
           the year,
       The secret window whence the world looks small and
           very dear.
       He sees as in a mirror on the monstrous twilight sea
       The crescent of his cruel ships whose name is mystery;
       They fling great shadows foe-wards, making Cross and
           Castle dark,
115    They veil the plumèd lions on the galleys of St. Mark;
       And above the ships are palaces of brown, black-
           bearded chiefs,
       And below the ships are prisons, where with multi-
           tudinous griefs,
       Christian captives sick and sunless, all a labouring race
           repines
       Like a race in sunken cities, like a nation in the mines.
120    They are lost like slaves that swat, and in the skies of
           morning hung
       The stairways of the tallest gods when tyranny was
           young.
       They are countless, voiceless, hopeless as those fallen
           or fleeing on
       Before the high Kings' horses in the granite of
           Babylon.
       And many a one grows witless in his quiet room in
           hell

125 Where a yellow face looks inward through the lattice of his cell,
And he finds his God forgotten, and he seeks no more a sign—
(*But Don John of Austria has burst the battle-line!*)
Don John pounding from the slaughter-painted poop,
Purpling all the ocean like a bloody pirate's sloop,
130 Scarlet running over on the silvers and the golds,
Breaking of the hatches up and bursting of the holds,
Thronging of the thousands up that labour under sea
White for bliss and blind for sun and stunned for liberty.
*Vivat Hispania!*
135 *Domino Gloria!*
Don John of Austria
Has set his people free!

Cervantes on his galley sets the sword back in the sheath
(*Don John of Austria rides homeward with a wreath.*)
140 And he sees across a weary land a straggling road in Spain,
Up which a lean and foolish knight forever rides in vain,
And he smiles, but not as Sultans smile, and settles back the blade....
(*But Don John of Austria rides home from the Crusade.*)

# Notes

By Dale Ahlquist and Peter Floriani

(The initial number refers to the line of the poem.)

1   "founts . . . in the courts of the sun": The fountains in the Sultan's palace.

2   "Soldan of Byzantium": Selim II (1524–1574), the Sultan of Constantinople (seat of the Turkish Ottoman Empire). "Soldan" is another word for "Sultan", and a more poetic one.

5   "crescent": The crescent is the symbol of the Muslims. It was adopted as the emblem of the Turkish Empire after the taking of Constantinople in 1453. Chesterton makes the Sultan's smile in the shape of a crescent.

6   "inmost sea of all the earth": The Mediterranean, with apologies to the Black Sea.

6   "shaken with his ships":

> The taking of Famagusta [a port on the island of Cyprus] in 1571 had therefore been planned as a stunning public demonstration of Turkish might—a preliminary to all-out war on other Venetian possessions. . . . By an ostentatious and perhaps unnecessary display of force, the Sultan was

making it clear that he still held command of the sea.... Sultan Selim could land an army within striking distance of Rome only if he had command of the sea. This is exactly what his attack on Cyprus ... had put at issue (Jack Beeching, *The Galleys at Lepanto* 174, 181).

7   "dared the white republics": The Italian city-states of Venice, Genoa, Florence, and, of course, the Papal States were all threatened by the Islamic forces.

8   "dashed the Adriatic round the Lion of the Sea": The winged lion of St. Mark is the emblem of Venice.

Ali, the Turkish admiral, was keeping up the pressure on Venice. In June [1571] he raided Crete. By attacking one Venetian island after another that summer, the Turks reasoned that they could compel Venice to disperse her galleys, some here, some there, so that the entire Holy League fleet would never arrive at Messina.... He had the armed force to land an expedition in Italy if he chose, a well-supplied battle fleet and an impregnable anchorage [at Lepanto].... The threat was unmistakable. If not this year then next, not only Venice and Rome but the kingdom of Naples and the island of Sicily, Spain's breadbasket, would all lie within striking distance of this immense Turkish fleet and its army (ibid., 187–89).

9–10   "the Pope ... called the kings of Christendom": Pope Pius V (1504–1572), a Dominican monk who was very holy and ascetic (and who was eventually canonized), was stunningly different from his Renaissance predecessors, who all came from the aristocratic class and were some of the most notoriously corrupt popes in history, and under whom Christendom splintered. There was "agony and loss" within Christian Europe, but the most immediate threat came from without: from the Muslim Turks.

> The new Pope, Pius V, was making valiant efforts to form a league "for the destruction and ruin of the Turk". . . . The essential political obstacle was still there. The two great Christian naval powers in the Mediterranean were Spain and Venice . . . but until now, the interests of Spain and Venice had never coincided. Indeed, they were chronically at odds. In Rome that year [1570], in the month of June, negotiations for a Holy League had officially begun. . . . The Pope was sure in his own mind that unless the Holy League had been made effective by the spring of 1571, the present chance of rebuffing Turkish aggression would be lost. Combining acts of financial generosity with words of passionate conviction, he laboured all winter to bring Spain and Venice closer—or, at least, to prevent their flying apart. . . . To place limits on the bickering between Venice and Spain, the Pope had done his best to involve other powers, not always with success. . . . The Pope had even gone so far as to seek help—of course in vain—from Ivan the Terrible (ibid., 122–23, 161, 167–68).

11   "cold queen of England": Elizabeth I of England (1533–1603), who is considered "cold" for a number of reasons. She was known for never revealing her feelings in public, and her apparent aloofness is why some thought she never married. But her calculating approach toward marriage *was* genuinely cold:

she regarded marriage as a diplomatic practice. She would periodically entertain the possibility of marriage whenever it would seem beneficial (that is, to form an alliance), but never followed through with it. Chesterton has her looking in the mirror, to paint her as self-absorbed and uncaring about the fate of Christian Europe. Ironically, although she offered no help whatsoever to the Holy League, she recognized the significance of the victory at Lepanto once the battle was won, and she ordered the Church of England, which she had established by law, to hold services of thanksgiving.

12    "The shadow of the Valois": Charles IX (1550–1574) was nominally King of France, but actually he was in the power of his mother, Catherine de Medici, the Duchess of Valois.

> When appealed to for help by the Pope in a personal letter, King Charles IX of France sent a cold, brief and negative reply. . . . The Spanish ambassador in Paris sent a warning to King Philip [of Spain] that "here in France, everyone is doing his best to prevent the League from taking place" (ibid., 167).

12    "yawning at the Mass": Indicates the indifferent attitude of Charles IX toward the Church and the Pope.

13    "evening isles fantastical": The West Indies and other islands in the West held by Spain, thus distracting Philip II's attention and resources away from the battle with the Turks in the Mediterranean.

14    "the Lord upon the Golden Horn": The Sultan's palace in Constantinople (modern-day Istanbul) overlooks an arm

of the Bosporus called "the Golden Horn", which is considered the most perfect harbor in the world.

14   "laughing in the sun": The Sultan laughs because Christendom is not united, England and France have no interest in opposing the Turks, and Venice is tied to them by trade agreements.

> Patiently following his strategy of dividing Venice from Spain, Sokolli the Grand Vizier let the Venetians know privately that a separate peace might always be possible.... Venice, of course, was playing a double game. "Peace is better for you than war," Sokolli reminded the Venetians paternally. "You cannot cope with the Sultan, who will take from you not only Cyprus alone, but other dependencies. As for your Christian League, we know full well how little love the Christian princes bear you. If you would but hold by the Sultan's robe, you might do what you want in Europe, and enjoy perpetual peace" (Beeching, *The Galleys at Lepanto*, 166, 169).

15   "Dim drums throbbing, in the hills half heard": A possible reference to Don John's gallant leadership against the Morisco uprising in the hills of the Alpujarras. In addition to learning his naval skills against Algerian corsairs, Don John learned how to be a great infantry commander in the Alpujarras. The Sultan had encouraged insurrection in the Alpujarras, but made no effort to support it, probably because the lines of communication would have been too long. Thus the Sultan paid scant attention to the uprising in the Alpujarras and the young commander learning the skills that would contribute to his success at Lepanto. If the uprising in the

Alpujarras had not been put down it could have very well led to the collapse of the Spanish kingdom, and the doom of Christendom. The Pope genuinely worried about this. Don John's leadership in defeating the Moriscos was crucial at the seige of Galera where the other commanders were afraid and distraught by the Morisco defenses.

16  "nameless throne . . . crownless prince": Don John of Austria (1547–1578) was the illegitimate son of the great Holy Roman Emperor Charles V (1500–1558). His mother was Barbara Blomberg of Ratisbon (which was then an Austrian city— thus Don John *of Austria*). Chesterton calls him "Don John", the anglicized version of "Don Juan" (there is no relation to the legendary lover of that name). Being of royal blood, he is a prince, but being illegitimate, he is without a royal title. Thus he has a "nameless throne". But he is the one who answers the Pope's call and turns out to be perfectly suited to do so.

> The thorniest problem of all was solved when the Pope carried his own audacious proposal for a supreme commander, capable from his rank and character of rising above the jealousies which last year had bedeviled Colonna's fleet, a war leader competent to win what no Christian admiral had ever yet won: a great sea battle against the Turks. At the age of twenty-four, the late Emperor Charles V's bastard son, Don John of Austria, had the fate of the civilized world placed in his hands, "in a war that concerned all Christendom." (Ibid., 170–71)

17  "a doubtful seat and half-attainted stall": Don John's corrupted ("attainted") royal lineage and ambiguous office. There is also a Chestertonian pun at work here. Don John's office ("stall") is half-attained (because he is only half-royal, halfway

23

to the throne), and also half-tainted (because he is half-common and illegitimate). There is also the reference to the Act of Attainder, where a person is found guilty without trial, which, of course, is the case with anyone born illegitimate, who is usually referred to by the derogatory epithet "bastard".

28  "tuckets": A flourish of trumpets.

32–33  "Love-light of Spain . . . Death-light of Africa": Don John as the last of the Crusaders is the pride and hope of Spain and is the threat of doom and death to the Islamic Empire, which includes the Moors of northern Africa.

36  "Mahound": Muhammad. Some sources say this name is used contemptuously, hence meaning an evil spirit.

38  "timeless houri's knees": Houri is pronounced HOO-ri or HOW-ri. In the Muslim paradise, the faithful were rewarded with the companionship of beautiful women throughout eternity. A "houri" is a "dark-eyed nymph".

40  "peacock gardens": A symbol of oriental luxuriousness, and, more importantly, a symbol of pride.

> After all, a peacock was an unusual thing to see in the front garden of a small suburban villa. . . .
> "What, for instance, can be the basis of objecting to peacocks' feathers?"
> Crundle was replying with a joyful roar that it was some infernal rubbish or other, when Gale, who had quickly slipped into a seat beside the man called Noel, interposed in a conversational manner.
> "I fancy I can throw a little light on that. I believe I found a trace of it in looking at some old illuminated manuscripts of the ninth or tenth

century. There is a very curious design, in a stiff Byzantine style, representing the two armies preparing for the war in heaven. But St. Michael is handing out spears to the good angels; while Satan is elaborately arming the rebel angels with peacocks' feathers."

Noel turned his hollow eyes sharply in the direction of the speaker. "That is really interesting," he said; "you mean it was all that old theological notion of the wickedness of pride?"

"Well, there's a whole peacock in the garden for you to pluck," cried Crundle in his boisterous manner, "if any of you want to go out fighting angels."

"They are not very effective weapons," said Gale gravely, "and I fancy that is what the artist in the Dark Ages must have meant. There seems to me to be something that rather hits the wrong imperialism in the right place, about the contrast in the weapon; the fact that the right side was arming for a real and therefore doubtful battle, while the wrong side was already, so to speak, handing out the palms of victory. You cannot fight anybody with the palms of victory" (GKC, "The House of the Peacock", *The Poet and the Lunatics*, 142, 149).

42  "his voice through all the garden": Muhammad calls upon every possible spiritual enemy of the Church.

43  "Azrael": In Jewish and Muslim religion, the angel of death. Jewish tradition has almost made Azrael an evil genius. In Muslim theology, as the angel of death, he will be the last to die, doing so on the second trumpet blast of the Archangel Gabriel.

43    "Ariel": The spirit of the air. The Hebrew word means "Lion of God". In Is 29:1 "Ariel" stands for Jerusalem. In later Jewish times, it is the name of a water sprite. Milton gives this name to a fallen spirit in *Paradise Lost*, Shakespeare to the spirit in *The Tempest*.

43    "Ammon": Or, "Amun", the highest god of the ancient Egyptians. This word is the root of the common chemical "ammonia" and countless other chemicals (such as amino acids), as the compound was first found in a gum said to distill from plants growing near the temple of Jupiter Ammon.

44    "Genii": Or, "jinn", the plural of "genius" or "genie", also spelled "jinni". A jinni is a nature spirit; in Muslim belief, one of a class of supernatural beings, subject to magic control.

45    "Multiplex of wing and eye": Characteristic of supernatural beings:

> "And the four living creatures had each of them
> six wings; and round about and within they are
> full of eyes" (Rev 4:8ab).

47    "When Solomon was king": According to Muslim legend, Solomon had a ring inscribed with the name of God which gave him control over demons and genii of the underworld. The following is from the Qur'an:

> 21:81. And (We made subservient) to Sulaiman
> the wind blowing violent, pursuing its course by
> his command to the land which We had blessed,
> and We are knower of all things.
> 27:16. And Sulaiman was Dawood's heir, and he
> said: O men! we have been taught the language of
> birds, and we have been given all things; most
> surely this is manifest grace.

27:17. And his hosts of the jinn and the men and the birds were gathered to him, and they were formed into groups.

(Sulaiman is Solomon; Dawood is David.)

49  "temples where the yellow gods shut up their eyes in scorn":

> No two ideals could be more opposite than a Christian saint in a Gothic cathedral and a Buddhist saint in a Chinese temple. The opposition exists at every point; but perhaps the shortest statement of it is that the Buddhist saint always has his eyes shut, while the Christian saint always has them very wide open. The Buddhist saint has a sleek and harmonious body, but his eyes are heavy and sealed with sleep. The mediaeval saint's body is wasted to its crazy bones, but his eyes are frightfully alive. There cannot be any real community of spirit between forces that produced symbols so different as that (GKC, *Orthodoxy*, *CW* 1:336).

51  "fallen skies ... evil hues ... eyeless creatures": A reference to Lucifer and his demons who fell from heaven. Muhammad has all the creatures of hell at his disposal. The sea is a fallen sky. Evil hues are the very colors that are not colors, that feed off the true and bold colors, but are weak and bloodless. The eyeless creatures of the depths symbolize those who love darkness rather than light because their deeds are evil (Jn 3:19).

53  "splendid sickness ... of the pearl": The pearl, while beautiful, is really a product of the oyster's sickness. It is formed around some foreign object in its body, usually a grain of

sand. Thus, for Chesterton, the pearl represents luxury wrought by corruption. The splendor of wealth is an abnormality, and it is, in reality, well-decorated dirt.

57   "bone of saint": Relics, which were considered holy by medieval Christians. Muhammad is calling for the destruction of all these relics. This was an effective method of destroying the faith and the whole culture supporting it, as English Catholics would know, since Henry VIII (1491–1547, ruled 1509–1547) had all the relics of saints destroyed under his rule, including those of St. Thomas à Becket at Canterbury Cathedral.

58   "Giaours": Pronounced "JOW-ers" to rhyme with "hours". Unbelievers, an insulting name used by Muslims for anyone not of their faith.

60   "We have set the seal of Solomon": The seal is the symbol on the ring, referred to above. This is Muhammad's claim that Solomon belongs to Islam and not to Judaism or Christianity, that Solomon's wisdom is theirs and not anyone else's.

63   "four hundred years ago": The time of the early Crusades. In the first Crusade the Christians conquered Jerusalem in 1099, and held the city for over eighty years. The Third Crusde nearly re-conquered Jerusalem in 1191, but failed.

64   "Kismet": A brotherly greeting among Muslims, but more importantly, Fate. Muhammad sees that the Christian threat to Islam is the exaltation of free will over the resignation to fate.

65   "Richard": Leader of the Third Crusade. Richard I Coeur de Lion (the Lion-Hearted) (1157–1199).

65  "Raymond": A leader of the First Crusade. Raymond IV, Count of Toulouse, (ca.1038–1105).

65  "Godfrey": Another leader of the First Crusade. Godfrey de Bouillon, Duke of Lower Lorraine, (1061–1100). He was elected King of Jerusalem, July 22, 1099, but refused to let himself be called a king.

> Curiously enough Godfrey seems to have been heroic even in those admirable accidents which are generally and perhaps rightly regarded as the trappings of fiction. Thus he was of heroic stature, a handsome red-bearded man of great personal strength and daring; and he was himself the first man over the wall of Jerusalem, like any boy hero in a boy's adventure story. But he was also, the realist will be surprised to hear, a perfectly honest man, and a perfectly genuine practicer of the theoretical magnanimity of knighthood. Everything about him suggests it; from his first conversion from the imperial to the papal (and popular) cause, to his great refusal of the kinghood of the city he had taken; "I will not wear a crown of gold where my Master wore a crown of thorns" (GKC, "The Meaning of the Crusade", *The New Jerusalem, CW* 20:366–67).

66  "It is he whose loss is laughter when he counts the wager worth": Chesterton has Muhammad recognizing the vital distinction between the Christian and the Islamic perspectives of the ultimate sacrifice, between the Christian martyr, "whose loss is laughter" and the cheerless and suicidal Islamic fanatic, who is simply betting the whole herd on a ticket to the peacock gardens. The difference between the

Christian and Muslim paradise is striking: Muhammad is in a sensual place, where what was forbidden on earth is now luxuriantly indulged in. Yet there is evidently no contentment. (There never is in sensuality.) Muhammad is pushing aside the lovely houris and kicking peacocks out of his way. For the Christian, on the other hand, heaven is to be in the presence of God, the sum of all hopes and happiness, the essence of fulfillment. It is perfect contentment, and it cannot even be imagined. The duties on earth are almost a joke in comparison. The pains on earth, even the pleasures on earth are a joke in comparison. Laughter is the recognition of the incongruity between the real and the ideal, and is an act of humility. The sneer, on the other hand, recognizes a temporal advantage, even if it is a temporary one, and it is an act of superiority (this poem begins with the Sultan's sneer). The martyr has the levity of true courage, whereas the person who commits suicide has only the despair of resignation.

> The recent stage of culture and criticism might very well be summed up as the men who smile criticising the men who laugh.... Therefore, in this modern conflict between the Smile and the Laugh, I am all in favour of laughing. Laughter has something in it in common with the ancient winds of faith and inspiration; it unfreezes pride and unwinds secrecy; it makes men forget themselves in the presence of something greater than themselves; something (as the common phrase goes about a joke) that they cannot resist (GKC, *The Common Man*, 157, 158–59).

> Now laughter is a thing that can be let go; laughter has in it a quality of liberty. But sorrow has in it by its very nature a quality of confinement;

pathos by its very nature fights with itself. Humour is expansive; it bursts outwards; the fact is attested by the common expression, "holding one's sides." But sorrow is not expansive (GKC, "Pickwick Papers", *Appreciations and Criticisms of the Works of Charles Dickens*, *CW* 15:252–53).

Let us follow for a moment the clue of the martyr and the suicide; and take the case of courage. No quality has ever so much addled the brains and tangled the definitions of merely rational sages. Courage is almost a contradiction in terms. It means a strong desire to live taking the form of a readiness to die. "He that will lose his life, the same shall save it," is not a piece of mysticism for saints and heroes. It is a piece of everyday advice for sailors or mountaineers. It might be printed in an Alpine guide or a drill book. This paradox is the whole principle of courage; even of quite earthly or quite brutal courage. A man cut off by the sea may save his life if he will risk it on the precipice. He can only get away from death by continually stepping within an inch of it (GKC, *Orthodoxy*, *CW* 1:297, quoting Mt 16:25).

67 "that our peace be on the earth": This line should be read: "that *our* peace be on the earth", that is, the "peace" represented by Islam. There are some who claim that the word "Islam" means "peace", but, even so, it is a purely Islamic peace. A more literal translation of the word means "submission to the will of Allah".

"If you would but hold by the Sultan's robe, you might do what you want in Europe, and enjoy perpetual peace" (Beeching, *The Galleys at Lepanto*, 169).

71    "Iberia": Spain. This is an example of a "synecdoche", a figure of speech in which the whole stands for a part, as the Iberian Peninsula also includes Portugal.

73    "Alcalar": Alcalá de Gudaira, a town in southwestern Spain, which was once a Moorish stronghold. The Moors were defeated by the Christians in 1246. Chesterton has Don John riding to the sea by way of the site of a famous victory over the Muslims, another reference that he is the last Crusader, and that like the first Crusades, this is a battle against Islamic aggression.

74    "St. Michael's on his Mountain": Mont St. Michel, a Benedictine Abbey on a rocky islet off the coast of France and sacred to St. Michael, patron of all battles where the forces of goodness must overcome the forces of evil.

> Mount St. Michael . . . stands among the sands of Normandy on the other side of the narrow seas. The first part of the sensation is that the traveller, as he walks the stony streets between the walls, feels that he is inside a fortress. But it is the paradox of such a place that, while he feels in a sense that he is in a prison, he also feels that he is on a precipice. The sense of being uplifted, and set on a high place, comes to him through the smallest cranny, or most accidental crack in rock or stone; it comes to him especially through those long narrow windows in the walls of the old fortifications; those slits in the stone through which the medieval archers used their bows and the medieval artists used their eyes, with even greater success. Those green glimpses of fields

32

far below or of flats far away, which delight us and yet make us dizzy (by being both near and far) when seen through the windows of Memling, can often be seen from the walls of Jerusalem. Then I remembered that in the same strips of medieval landscape could be seen always, here and there, a steep hill crowned with a city of towers. And I knew I had the mystical and double pleasure of seeing such a hill and standing on it. A city that is set upon a hill cannot be hid; but it is more strange when the hill cannot anywhere be hid, even from the citizen in the city (GKC, *The New Jerusalem*, *CW* 20:225–26).

78–79    "He shakes his lance of iron . . . The noise is gone through Normandy." St. Michael, who fought Lucifer and all his angels, now comes to thwart the fallen spirits that have been summoned by Muhammad. But no one from the North comes to his aid; lines 80–84 explain why.

80    "The North is full of tangled things and texts and aching eyes": A reference to the Protestant myopic focus on biblical texts and translations. The "tangled things" are all the heretical ideas that would flow out of Germany, ironically undermining the sacred scripture itself with textual criticism and producing all the twisted philosophies from Kant to Hegel to Nietzsche to the Nazis—the anti-Christian ideas that would infiltrate and undermine all of Christian Europe.

81    "dead is all the innocence of anger and surprise": Chesterton concedes that the initial Protestant rebellion was innocent, "good men who had good reason to be wrong" ("The Party Question", in GKC, *The Queen of Seven Swords*). The initial anger was innocent, but that is now gone. It is now merely a fruitless feud. But more profound than the loss of

33

innocent anger is the loss of innocent surprise, for the first effect of shaking the Church was to discover some of its forgotten truths. When truth is no longer a surprise, when it has lost its wonder, it is in danger not only of being ignored, but of being lost. For Chesterton, truth is always best conveyed as a surprise.

82   "Christian killeth Christian in a narrow dusty room": The growing conflict, sometimes bloody, between Catholics and Protestants. Specifically, it may be a reference to the wars between the Catholics and Huguenots in France. The infamous St. Bartholomew's Day Massacre took place on August 24, 1572, during the reign of Charles IX, although it is reported that he did not order it. The "narrow dusty room" possibly refers to the murder of Admiral de Coligny, leader of the Calvinist Party, at the start of the massacre.

83   "Christian dreadeth Christ that hath a newer face of doom": A reference to Calvinism and the doctrine of predestination. Chesterton said that the Calvinist "substituted a God who wished to damn people for a God who wished to save them" (*Sidelights*, *CW*, 21:563).

84   "Christian hateth Mary that God kissed in Galilee": For Chesterton, perhaps the supreme example of the tangled things coming out of the North with the disruption of Christianity is the Protestant rejection of the Church's historical veneration of the Blessed Virgin Mary in her unique role as the Mother of God. The "kiss" is a reference not only to the miracle of the Virgin Birth, but to the Annunciation, when God's messenger, the Angel Gabriel, knelt before a woman and said, "Hail, full of Grace" (Luke 1:28). In contrast, before the battle Don John has his entire army pray the Rosary.

86 "eclipse": The sea was shrouded in fog on the morning of the battle.

89 *"Domino gloria!"*: Latin for "Glory to the Lord!"

90–91 "Don John of Austria / Is shouting to the ships":

> Crucifix in hand, Don John proceeded in a *fregata* along one wing, to rectify order in the line of battle and hearten the men. Luis de Requeséns did the same duty on the other wing. To one ship's company after another, Don John's clear and almost boyish voice pealed out with the same assurance: "My children, we are here to conquer or die. In death or victory, you will win immortality" (Beeching, *The Galleys at Lepanto*, 210).

92 "King Philip's in his closet": King Philip II of Spain (1527–1598), son of Emperor Charles V and half brother to Don John of Austria.

92 "the Fleece about his neck": Order of the Golden Fleece, established in 1430 by Philip I (Philip the Good), grandfather to Philip II, to celebrate the joining of Flanders and Burgundy. The confraternity of the Golden Fleece still exists, with King Juan Carlos of Spain as one patron.

93 *"Don John of Austria is armed upon the deck"*: He had more weapons at his disposal than merely physical ones:

> Whether free man or galley slave, each Christian aboard had been given a rosary. As the naked galley slaves, hauling on their oars, moved past the mole at the harbour mouth, they saw there the

papal nuncio in his cardinal's robes, immobile, alone, holding up his arms to bless them until the last ship was gone (ibid., 194–95).

95   "little dwarfs": Spanish royalty often employed dwarfs as companions for children, or even as substitutes for children. There are examples of this illustrated in paintings by the great Spanish court painter Velasquez. If that seems a little perverse, that is probably Chesterton's intention.

96–100   "a crystal phial ... death is in the phial": Poison. Chesterton subscribes to the legend that King Philip actually murdered Don John, his heroic half brother, out of jealousy and distrust. There is little evidence to support this idea, and most Catholics consider it a Protestant slander. But it is interesting that Chesterton gives it credence. Philip took great pains to ensure that everyone referred to Don John as "Your Excellency" rather than the royal "Your Highness", a not-too-subtle way of ensuring that all would know he was an illegitimate son in the Royal House. After the celebrated victory at Lepanto, Don John was given a series of seemingly impossible tasks by Philip, all of which he accomplished in spite of being given no support. Ultimately, he was appointed by Philip to govern the Netherlands, which in some minds, was not much different from exile, ("Flanders, that graveyard of eminent reputations", O'Connell, *The Counter Reformation 1559–1610*). The Netherlands had rebelled against Spanish rule and had also rejected the Catholic Faith. It was a thankless task for Don John to go there and try to straighten things out, and though he worked hard to negotiate a settlement with the rebels, he lost Philip's confidence when the pact was not recognized by the provinces of Holland and Zeeland. Shortly thereafter, in 1578, Don John met a mysterious and untimely death. Though it is usually attributed to typhoid, he expired so quickly that some suspected poison. Whether or not Philip had anything to do with the death of Don John, it is fairly certain that Philip arranged the murder of Don John's secretary, Juan de Escobedo, a fact that lends support to the legend that he also had Don John killed.

98   "his face is as a fungus": Chesterton's uncomplimentary portrait of King Philip as a diseased and paranoid recluse may be disputed by some, but it is not without supporting evidence. His "health was habitually poor. He was rarely out of the doctor's hand" and he endured "long days of ghastly suffering", (R. Trevor Davies, *The Golden Century of Spain 1501–1621*). He never left his province and seldom left his palace. Though Philip was well loved by the Spanish and is considered a hero of the Counter-Reformation, he was notoriously suspicious of everyone around him, and many of those closest to him ultimately suffered disgrace, including, of course, Don John. Chesterton is certainly no fan of the man who launched the attack of the Armada against England in 1588. He believed that the reason Philip did not give his full and complete support to the Pope's call for arms against the Turks at Lepanto was that he was saving his resources to attack England. While Chesterton would have preferred England becoming Catholic again, he would not have wanted it to be brought about by England being conquered by a Spanish attack. He preferred the elegant solution of Don John marrying Mary, Queen of Scots, which was in fact what Don John had intended to do before he met with his untimely death. (See GKC's essay on this topic below, pp. 95–117.) In any case, there is still a certain accuracy in Chesterton's vivid contrast between the two half brothers: King Philip, "in his closet" (l. 92), *was* as far away from the battle as possible, wearing the "Fleece about his neck" (l. 92), while Don John *was* "*armed upon the deck*" (l. 93), in the thick of the fighting.

101–7   "But Don John of Austria has fired upon the Turk
... loosed the cannonade": For the sake of safety during fog
(during the days of October 5 and 6) Don John had issued
orders that no one was to fire a gun.

> From the crescent of Turkish ships as under sail they
> moved closer to their Christian enemy came yells,
> random shots, religious ululations of defiance.
> Gongs and huge cymbals clashed, conches blared:
> the Turkish uproar was meant to shake the nerves.
> From the ships of the Holy League, not a shot had
> yet been fired—this prolonged silence was omi-
> nous. ... An accepted convention of sea warfare in
> those days laid down that flagships do not engage.
> But Ali and Don John, as if their minds were set on
> a duel, were seen to be heading directly towards one
> another. The first gunshot of the battle from the
> Christian side—breaking the imposed silence—
> was fired by Don John at extravagantly long range,
> straight at Ali, like a personal challenge (Beeching,
> *The Galleys at Lepanto*, 212).

108   "The Pope was in his chapel before day or battle broke":

> Pius V had prayed for the expedition almost un-
> ceasingly ... prescribing public devotions and pri-
> vate fasts, and at the very hour that the contest
> was raging, the procession of the rosary in the
> church of the Minerva was pouring forth peti-
> tions for victory (Thurston and Attwater, *Butler's
> Lives of the Saints*, May 5 [St. Pius V] 2:235–36).

Note that the "church of the Minerva" is Santa Maria sopra
Minerva in Rome, where the Holy League had been

proclaimed on the feast of St. Thomas Aquinas, March 7, 1571 ("sopra", meaning "above", as the church was built over the temple of the Roman goddess).

110    "hidden room in a man's house where God sits all the year": A reference to the Blessed Sacrament inside the tabernacle on the altar in the Pope's chapel.

> It is rather as if a man had found an inner room in the very heart of his own house, which he had never suspected; and seen a light from within (GKC, *The Everlasting Man*, *CW* 2:316–17).

111    "the world looks small and very dear":

> For me all good things come to a point, swords for instance. So finding the boast of the big cosmos so unsatisfactory to my emotions I began to argue about it a little; and I soon found that the whole attitude was even shallower than could have been expected. According to these people the cosmos was one thing since it had one unbroken rule. Only (they would say) while it is one thing it is also the only thing there is. Why, then, should one worry particularly to call it large? There is nothing to compare it with. It would be just as sensible to call it small. A man may say, "I like this vast cosmos, with its throng of stars and its crowd of varied creatures." But if it comes to that why should not a man say, "I like this cosy little cosmos, with its decent number of stars and as neat a provision of live stock as I wish to see"? One is as good as the other; they are both mere sentiments. It is mere sentiment to rejoice that the sun is larger than the earth; it is quite as sane a sentiment to

rejoice that the sun is no larger than it is. A man chooses to have an emotion about the largeness of the world: why should he not choose to have an emotion about its smallness?

It happened that I had that emotion. When one is fond of anything one addresses it by diminutives, even if it is an elephant or a life-guardsman. The reason is, that anything, however huge, that can be conceived of as complete, can be conceived of as small. If military moustaches did not suggest a sword or tusks a tail, then the object would be vast because it would be immeasurable. But the moment you can imagine a guardsman you can imagine a small guardsman. The moment you really see an elephant you can call it "Tiny." If you can make a statue of a thing you can make a statuette of it. These people professed that the universe was one coherent thing; but they were not fond of the universe. But I was frightfully fond of the universe and wanted to address it by a diminutive. I often did so; and it never seemed to mind. Actually and in truth I did feel that these dim dogmas of vitality were better expressed by calling the world small than by calling it large. For about infinity there was a sort of carelessness which was the reverse of the fierce and pious care which I felt touching the pricelessness and the peril of life. They showed only a dreary waste; but I felt a sort of sacred thrift. For economy is far more romantic than extravagance. To them stars were an unending income of halfpence; but I felt about the golden sun and the silver moon as a schoolboy feels if he has one sovereign and one shilling (GKC, *Orthodoxy*, *CW* 1:266–67).

111–12    "secret window. . . . / He sees as in a mirror": By several accounts the Pope had a vision of the battle and was aware of the victorious outcome before the actual reports reached him.

> Meanwhile the Pope himself was conversing on business with some of his cardinals; but on a sudden he turned from them abruptly, *opened a window*, and remained for some time with his eyes fixed on the sky. Then, closing the casement, he said, "This is not a moment in which to talk business: let us give thanks to God for the victory He has granted to the arms of the Christians" (Thurston and Attwater, *Butler's Lives of the Saints*, May 5 [St. Pius V], 2:236, [emphasis added]).

113    "crescent of his cruel ships":

> The usual Turkish battle formation was the crescent—which had for the Turks both a patriotic and a religious significance—with extending wings curved forwards to outflank, enfold and crush Ali and his commanders would follow tradition. But in the Holy League fleet much thought had gone into devising a novel battle order, which would take full advantage of fire power. . . . a *cruciform* formation had been worked out which would bring to bear the League's advantage in gunnery against the Turk's long crescent (Beeching, *The Galleys at Lepanto*, 196–97, 206 [emphasis added]).

113    "whose name is mystery": It is an Islamic precept that Allah is "The Hidden One". Even his hiddenness is hidden. Perhaps, too, Chesterton is referring to Babylon (as he does in lines 120–24). "And on her forehead a name was written:

A mystery: Babylon the great, the mother of the fornications and the abominations of the earth" (Rev 17:5).

114    "They fling great shadows foe-wards": "Foe-wards" is a marvelous play on words—forward and towards the foe. In the morning of October 7, the Turks were due east of the Holy League and sailing west:

> The Turks had left their safe refuge at Lepanto, and were sailing out to sea with a following wind.... Ali's battle line.... was a thousand meters longer than Don John's, reaching without a break from the shoal water northwards on the mountainous Albanian shore, to the shallows southward, along the coast of the Morea. His fleet therefore blocked entirely the entrance to the Gulf (Beeching, *The Galleys at Lepanto*, 209–10).

114    "Cross and Castle": The coat of arms of Aragon and of Castile on the Spanish ships. Also, the line points to the fact that the formations of the ships literally formed a cross and a crescent.

115    "galleys of St. Mark": The Venetian ships. St. Mark, symbolized by the lion, is the patron saint of Venice. The symbol of the lion was on the Venetian ships.

118    "Christian captives": These were galley slaves in the Turkish fleet:

> In Ali's fleet there were upwards of 14,000 galley slaves owing Christian allegiance. The risk of death for all of them, and yet the chance of freedom, was coming at every moment closer (ibid., 211).

118 "repines": to "repine" means "to feel or express dejection or discontent; to complain; grumble".

120 "swat": An obsolete form of "sweated".

121–23 "stairways of the tallest gods when tyranny was young. . . . the granite of Babylon": The word "Babylon" indicates that this is a reference to the time of Israel's captivity in Babylon, when as slaves they were forced to bow down to huge idols ("the tallest gods"). The Christian slaves here share in the long procession of slavery throughout history.

126 "he seeks no more a sign": Chesterton vividly portrays the hopelessness of the Christian captives in the Sultan's galleys. But just when it appeared that all hope was gone for the Christian slaves at Lepanto, there *was* a sign: the sudden shift of the wind that utterly turned the advantage from the Turks to the Holy League:

> While Ali's ships visibly lost momentum, all along Don John's battle line, lateen sails were being shaken out along spars. They filled as if from a mighty and confident breath. As they heard or half heard the chaplains' insistent voices, there were few in the League fleet who doubted that God had intervened (Beeching, *The Galleys at Lepanto*, 212).

128 "Don John pounding from the slaughter-painted poop": The poop is a raised structure above the main deck and located at the stern (rear) of a ship or galley.

> A third rush had carried the Sardinian boarding party . . . all the way to Ali's poop . . . Ali at last was struck in the forehead by an arquebus bullet. . . . By two in the afternoon, with the Turkish

admiral killed and his flagship taken and gutted, Don John could afford to wipe the bloody sweat from his eyes (ibid., 214).

129 "sloop": A nautical term for a type of sailing vessel with a single mast, but also for a ship rigged with guns.

130 "the silvers and the golds":

> In the hold of the Turkish flagship they discovered an incredible treasure—which they kept for themselves. Ali had brought his entire personal fortune with him—150,000 gold sequins—rather than leave it behind in Constantinople and risk having it confiscated should he happen to displease Sultan Selim (Beeching, *The Galleys at Lepanto*, 214).

132–33 "Thronging of the thousands up that labour under sea / White for bliss and blind for sun and stunned for liberty":

> By four on that Sunday afternoon, 7 October 1571, the battle of Lepanto was over. The specific menace which had brought the Holy League fleet into being—the Turkish battle fleet—had been destroyed. . . . More than 12,000 Christian galley slaves, of whom over 2000 were Spanish—all victims of kidnapping raids in past years around the Mediterranean—were now free men (ibid., 220).

134 "*Vivat Hispania!*": Latin for "Long Live Spain!"

138 "Cervantes": Miguel de Cervantes (1547–1616) was the author of *Don Quixote*, Spain's great satirical classic. He was wounded in the battle and lost the use of his left hand.

139   "*wreath*": The sign of victory, the symbolic reward to the victor in battle.

141   "a lean and foolish knight": This is Cervantes' famous character, Don Quixote.

141   "forever rides in vain":

> Cervantes . . . wrote a whole novel to show that it was nonsense to expect any adventures in this life, when his own life had been simply crammed with adventures. He seemed to smile Spain's chivalry away, when he had actually been risking his life for that chivalry and driving its Paynim enemies away. At Lepanto he was the first to leap, sword in hand, on to the galley of the Sultan—a thing obviously out of a boy's novelette. The first satirist of crusading romances was one of the last crusaders (GKC, *Illustrated London News*, Dec. 6, 1919 [*CW* 31:574]).

Note: "Paynim" is a seldom-used word to refer to pagan or non-Christian religions, but used by modern writers usually to refer to middle-eastern religions such as Islam.

There is also an allusion here to Lord Byron's *Don Juan*:

> Cervantes smiled Spain's chivalry away:
>   A single laugh demolish'd the right arm
> Of his own country:—seldom, since that day,
>   Has Spain had heroes. While Romance could charm,
> The world gave ground before her bright array;
>   And therefore have his volumes done such harm,
> That all glory, as a composition,
> Was dearly purchased by his land's perdition.
>         (Canto the Thirteenth [1823], stanza 11)

> There are two types of men who can laugh when
> they are alone. One might almost say the man
> who does it is either very good or very bad. You
> see, he is either confiding the joke to God or con-
> fiding it to the devil. But anyhow he has an inner
> life. Well, there really is a kind of man who con-
> fides the joke to the devil. He does not mind if
> nobody sees the joke; if nobody can safely be al-
> lowed even to know the joke. The joke is enough
> in itself, if it is sufficiently sinister and malignant
> (GKC "The Worst Crime in the World", *The Pen-
> guin Complete Father Brown*, 550).

143 *"Don John of Austria rides home from the Crusade"*: The
Battle of Lepanto has been called "the last battle of the last
crusade" by several sources, including O'Connell's history
of the Counter-Reformation. Chesterton uses the Crusade
imagery throughout the poem, from lines 9 and 10, where
the Pope appeals to "the kings of Christendom for swords
about the Cross", to Muhammad's references to Richard,
Raymond, and Godfrey and so on. The last Crusade was a
successful one for Christendom.

"Our Lady of Victory" is a reference to the Battle of
Lepanto. Interestingly enough, another surprising version of
Our Lady played a role at Lepanto. The second archbishop
of Mexico, Don Fray Alonso de Montufar, had a small re-
production of the Sacred Image of Our Lady of Guadalupe
made and, after touching it to the original, sent it to King
Philip of Spain in 1570. The archbishop knew of the im-
pending battle and asked that the image accompany the Holy
League, as he believed that it would work a miracle as the
original image had so many times in Mexico. The image

was mounted in the cabin of Admiral Giovanni Andrea Doria. It was Andrea Doria's fleet that was under the heaviest attack from the Turks when the wind suddenly shifted, changing the momentum of the battle and leading to the decisive victory by the Holy League.

> Pope St. Pius V in 1572 ordered an annual commemoration of our Lady of Victory to be made to implore God's mercy on His Church and all the faithful, and to thank Him for His protection and numberless benefits, particularly for His having delivered Christendom from the arms of the infidel Turks by the sea victory at Lepanto in the previous year, a victory which seemed a direct answer to the prayers and processions of the rosary confraternities at Rome made while the battle was actually being fought. A year later Pope Gregory XIII changed the name of the observance to that of the Rosary, fixing it for the first Sunday in October (the day of Lepanto). . . . Pope Clement XI decreed that the feast of the Holy Rosary should be observed throughout the western Church. The feast is now kept on the date of the battle of Lepanto, October 7 (Thurston and Attwater, *Butler's Lives of the Saints*, October 7 [Our Lady of the Rosary], 4:48).

# Commentary

*Don John of Austria*

# The Background

## By Brandon Rogers

G. K. Chesterton described the state of Europe in the middle of the sixteenth century as being "in one of its recurring periods of division and disease". I cannot think of a better description of that period in history in so few words. Europe at the time of the Battle of Lepanto in October of 1571 was both divided and diseased: divided by religious quarrels and an explosion of sects with creeds denying the authority of the established Christian Church, and diseased with both excessive worldliness still flowing from the Renaissance and an excessive and superstitious austerity growing in opposition to it.

Italy was perhaps the most "worldly" of the nations in Christendom at the time; where the Renaissance had first sprung its vibrant flowers the effects were lingering longest. In the various Italian states, Machiavellian politics were the order of the day, and the leading figures in much of Italian society were preoccupied with the preservation and expansion of their commercial interests. Venice was perhaps the most striking example of this, since it was a large city situated in an area unsuitable for agriculture supported almost entirely by international trade on the Mediterranean Sea. However, the Papal States and the Vatican itself were also not immune to the culture surrounding them. In many ways the popes since the Renaissance had actually helped to foster the sensual opulence and secretive politics that surrounded them.

France, perhaps more than any other European nation at the time, was in the midst of a violent internal religious conflict that had been fought on and off for almost a decade. Religion was not the only issue on which battles were being waged; many of the aristocracy, as well as the commercial interests in cities and towns, saw an opportunity in the civil disturbances to check the power of the French monarchy, which had been steadily increasing since the Middle Ages. The government of the nation itself, nominally ruled by King Charles IX, was ruled *de facto* by Charles' mother, Catherine de Medici, a daughter of the powerful Italian Medici family. Her attempts to diffuse the religious fighting within France by compromise were largely unsuccessful, and at the time that the Turks appeared most threatening to Europe on the Mediterranean, France was ill equipped to turn a unified front outward to meet any threat.

The kingdom of Spain, which also included at this time parts of France, Italy, and Belgium, as well as the Netherlands, was ruled by Philip II, son of Emperor Charles V. Philip was a devoutly Catholic but painfully suspicious ruler who was obsessed with personally managing every detail of his entire empire. Philip had inherited, arguably, the most powerful empire in Europe, but struggled to keep his geographically dispersed territories under a firm central authority greatly taxed his resources. Philip had also intensified the workings of the Spanish Inquisition, and much of his personal energy and his government's revenue were expended merely maintaining the status quo throughout his reign. Spain was also troubled by a large Muslim population in the South, which remained even after the Moors had been defeated two generations earlier. In November of 1570—less than a year before the Battle of Lepanto—the Spanish had finally put down an almost two-year-long revolt of Muslim "Moriscoes" in Granada.

In different ways, both England and Germany were preoccupied with internal developments. Elizabeth I in England was concerned with solidifying the newly formed Church of England and suppressing the shrinking but persistent pockets of resistance to the new political and religious order. Germany was growing accustomed to its own religious divisions. Although Charles V had roundly defeated a coalition of Protestant princes at Mühlberg in 1546, the spread of their Protestant religious doctrines had continued almost without slowing, and the Peace of Augsburg in 1555 had given official recognition to the Protestant states. The German princes, whether Catholic or Protestant, had settled into an uneasy truce for the time being and were occupied with dividing or defending the lands they had gained following the confiscation of Church property.

In stark contrast to "diseased and divided" Europe, the Turkish Ottoman Empire was, to all outward appearances, remarkably strong and unified. In 1453 the Turks had taken Constantinople, effectively completing their conquest of the remains of the Christian Byzantine Empire. By the first part of the sixteenth century, under the Sultan Suleiman the Magnificent, they began pressuring Europe on the Mediterranean as well as on Europe's eastern frontiers, having ransacked and subdued much of the Balkans, Hungary, and Wallachia (now Romania) and threatening Vienna in 1529.

After the death of Suleiman the Magnificent, Selim II ascended to the throne of Sultan in 1566. The Ottoman Empire over which Selim II came to power stretched all along the northern coast of Africa from modern Algeria to the Nile Delta, and included the Sinai Peninsula and the entire strip along the eastern Mediterranean coast, including what is now Israel, Lebanon, and Syria, as well as Turkey, Greece, and most of modern Romania, Hungary, and the Balkans.

Selim, though not particularly ambitious by nature, was under pressure to further expand the reaches of his empire. Every Ottoman Sultan was expected to bring at least one foreign state under Islamic rule during his reign.

Selim II was intent on fulfilling his obligation to expand the empire's territory, and much of Europe was trembling with fear. Since Selim's predecessor Suleiman had begun his expansion into eastern Europe in 1521, with the exception of the successful defense of Vienna in 1529, no major Turkish force had been defeated in living memory, and the Turks had a propensity for garish displays of power and cruelty in battle as well as on civilian populations after a victory. Europe gained a small confidence boost when, in a surprising defeat, Selim's forces unsuccessfully attempted to take the island of Malta in 1565. Chafed by this failure, Selim landed a much larger force on the Venetian-controlled island of Cyprus in 1570, conquering the defenses at Nicosia and Famagusta and making a gory spectacle of the latter city's Venetian governor, flaying him alive. As the summer of 1571 progressed, the Turkish fleet began raiding Venetian islands in the Adriatic, and the signs were clear that an attack on Italy was imminent.

In this seemingly dire situation there seemed to be only one light that shone brightly in "diseased and divided" Europe, and that was Pope Pius V. Elected pope in 1566, Pius V seemed the culmination of a quiet but rapid reformation in the papacy that, starting with Pope Paul III, brought true religious fervor and leadership back to the very top of the Catholic Church. Gone was the Renaissance worldliness and concern with secular affairs; Pius V knew that the most important issues of his day were the threats of Protestant heresies dividing Europe and the threat of the Muslim Turks conquering it, and that the victory in these struggles would only be won by utter reliance on the power and mercy of God.

Pius V was elected to the papacy right on the heels of the Turkish assault on Malta, and the air of tension and dread of the Turkish fleet was palpable throughout the Mediterranean. The Turkish threat was felt most immediately by Spain and Italy, and much to the new Pope's consternation both countries were jealously guarding their own interests and seemed almost completely unwilling to cooperate with one another. As the spring of 1571 approached, almost five years of pleading on the part of Pius V for Europe to unite in opposition to the threat of the Turkish fleet seemed without effect; King Philip of Spain had pledged only a few ships to the Pope's cause, and the Republic of Venice (then Italy's primary naval power) was stalling.

Pius understood the tremendous importance of resisting the aggressive expansion of the Turks better than any of his contemporaries appear to have. He understood that the real battle being fought was spiritual; a clash of creeds was at hand, and the stakes were the very existence of the Christian West. The piety and religious zeal that Pius brought to the papacy were perfectly suited to the crisis at hand, and Pius turned to the faithful under his charge for prayers and supplications to God. On March 7, 1571—exactly seven months before the Battle of Lepanto was fought—the Holy League was formed by Spain, Venice, and the Papal States of the Pope himself, each pledging a certain number of ships and men to the fleet to meet the Turks at sea. The Pope ordered more prayers and fasts for the success of the League, and, in particular, stressed the importance of one prayer: the Holy Rosary.

The Pope had personally and successfully advocated to place leadership of the Holy League's fleet in the hands of Don John of Austria. Don John was half brother to King Philip of

Spain, but it was his own reputation for valor, honesty, and military skill that recommended him. Don John also understood the stakes at hand. As Jack Beeching writes in *The Galleys at Lepanto*, Don John knew "he had been given the task of fighting a total war against another system of ideas—historically the hardest of all wars to win" (p. 197).

As the Holy League's fleet sailed out to meet the Turks in the late summer of 1571, all the ears of Europe were listening for news of their success—or failure. Echoing the Pope's exhortations to the faithful at home, the Holy League was also imploring the intercession of the Mother of God: each Christian in the League's fleet had been given a rosary before the fleet sailed from Messina. They sailed eventually into the Gulf of Lepanto and to meet the Turkish fleet on October 7, 1571, in (as G. K. Chesterton rightfully puts it) "one of the most splendid and appalling battles that ever stained the sea or smoked to the sun" (see below, p. 93). The Turkish fleet, with the wind at their backs, sailed confidently out to meet the Christians.

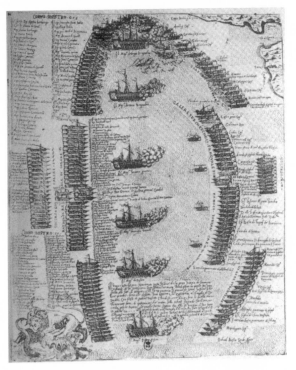

*A plan of the battle of Lepanto from an original document held in the Bibliothèque Nationale.*

# The Battle

By Melvin (Buzz) Kriesel, Colonel, U.S. Army (Retired)

The mighty armada formed by the Holy League had been lying at anchor since October 5, 1571. Foul winds and heavy fog had forced the fleet to stay in the harbor at Viscanto off the coast of Greece. It was the largest Christian force ever assembled, with 208 war galleys and seventy-six smaller craft manned by Venetian, Spanish, Genoese, Portuguese, and papal crews. More than thirty thousand soldiers packed the galley decks—another fifty thousand men were crammed below decks manning oars.

Its improbable admiral, the twenty-four-year-old Don John of Austria, led the Christian fleet. He was the bastard son of Emperor Charles V and half brother of Phillip II, the reigning King of Spain. Pope Pius V personally selected the youthful prince to lead the often fractious, always squabbling Holy League. Pius V had immediately sensed that Don John was "someone who in council would rise above pettiness and envy, who in battle would lead without flinching". The Holy Father blessed the young admiral and told him, "Charles V gave you life. I will give you honor and greatness" (Beeching, p. 187).

Pius V ordered the Holy League to advance south into the Gulf of Patras to seek out the Ottoman fleet, reported to be lying at anchor in the fortified harbor of Lepanto. The Ottoman fleet was fresh from its recent victory at Cyprus. Sultan Selim II was now assembling the men and ships necessary to sack Rome. In their advance throughout the Mediterranean, the Turks called Rome "the Red Apple". It was ripe, bright, and full of plunder. Pius V was certain the attack would take place the following year. He was convinced that the only chance to repel such an attack was to assemble as large a fleet as possible and engage the Turks at sea, rather than sit and wait for them to advance on Rome. He also knew that if Rome fell, all of Europe would fall after it. His strategy was twofold. He had both a physical and a spiritual plan of attack. He was counting on the Turkish fleet accepting the Holy League's challenge: "I take it for certain that the Turks, swollen by their victories, will wish to take on our fleet, and God—have the pious presentiment—will give us victory" (ibid., p. 187). And, most importantly, he knew that he was fighting a holy war, and that a holy war required holy men: "I am taking up arms against the Turks, but the only thing that can help me is the prayers of priests of pure life" (ibid., p. 182). In Don John, the Pope had a commander who shared perfectly his faith and philosophy. According to Beeching:

> Don John was clear in his own mind as to the terms on which Islamic aggression must be fought.... He had been given the task of fighting a total war against another system of ideas— historically, the hardest of all wars to win.... It followed that in the ships of the Holy League blasphemy or any other kind of religious doubt, openly expressed, had to be treated as sedition. The impending battle could be won only by men who were unanimous (ibid., p. 197).

The Pope might not have been so confident had he known the actual size of the Ottoman fleet anchored at Lepanto. There were over one hundred thousand men, many of them Janissaries, the most formidable infantrymen of their age, poised for an attack on Christendom. An Ottoman fleet of over three hundred major war galleys and eighty assorted gun ships ensured that the coming battle would be the largest galley fight in naval history. Ironically, it would prove that the age of the oared ship was already past.

On Sunday, October 7, 1571, Don John ordered the Christian fleet to weigh anchor and move south to seek out the Turkish fleet. However, no galley sailed until the Catholic priests who were serving as chaplains on each galley finished celebrating a predawn mass. The priests represented the major religious orders of the faith: Capuchins, Dominicans, Jesuits, and Theatines. They granted each man in the fleet the general absolution declared by the Pope to all who served and died on this fateful day.

The day did not begin well for the Christian fleet as it moved through the early morning fog and mist. The rowers manning the banks of heavy oars had to struggle to keep the galleys in motion against stiff headwinds blowing up the coast of Greece. Bosons with whips paced the catwalks, ready to lash any man not thought to be pulling his weight. With great difficulty, the fleet worked its way south and rounded into the narrows of the Gulf of Patras.

As the Christian advance guard entered the gulf, it saw a gigantic force of Ottoman war galleys bearing from the east in full battle array. The Ottoman fleet commanded by Muezzinzade Ali Pasha had left its fortified harbor at Lepanto and was now anchored at the mouth of the gulf, awaiting news of the advancing Christians. Ali Pasha ordered his fleet to take up battle stations as soon as lookouts posted high on the peaks guarding the northern shore signaled that the Christian fleet was entering the gulf. Less than fifteen miles of open water now separated the forces of Christendom from an Islamic multitude that stretched shore to shore across the gulf.

Ali Pasha's war galleys were deployed in a gigantic crescent. In the center, the Christians could see Ali Pasha's green and gold battle pennant streaming high on the mast of his flagship, the *Sultana*. The Islamic pennant was covered with verses from the Qur'an and emblazoned with the name "Allah" embroidered 28, 900 times in gold calligraphy. It was the banner of the Sultan and one of the Islamic treasures of Mecca. The Prophet himself had carried the sacred symbol—it had never been captured in battle.

Don John signaled that he intended to engage. He ordered that the battle pennant of the Holy League be run up the mast of his command ship, the *Real*. The great banner, blessed and given to the Holy League by Pius V, unfurled to display a gigantic cross. The consecrated banner was heralded by a great shout from the soldiers of the Holy League who until this time had been ominously quiet. By contrast, the Muslim fleet was advancing in a cacophony of sound— ululating war cries and prayers, random shots, clashing gongs and banging cymbals, and blaring bugles, all meant to attack the enemy's courage and shatter his nerve.

The war galleys of the Holy League continued to struggle with a head wind, while the galley slaves of the Ottoman fleet rested at their oars. Priests on the Christian galleys moved about the decks with raised crucifixes, blessing the men and hearing final confessions. Every man on board, whether slave or free, held a rosary and implored the Blessed Virgin for victory in the coming battle. Their prayers joined those of countless Christians throughout Europe who were also praying the Rosary, as requested by the Pope.

Don John climbed into a small galliot and rowed across the line of his advancing armada, calling out to his men, "You have come to fight the battle of the Cross—to conquer or to die. But whether you die or conquer, do your duty this day, and you will secure a glorious immortality" (*Atlantic*

*Monthly*, Dec. 1857, p. 139). Then, he went back to the *Real* and knelt at the bow, eyes raised to heaven, humbly praying that the Almighty bless his people with victory. Across the fleet, officers and men followed his example by dropping to their knees. With eyes fixed on the consecrated banner streaming from the mast of the *Real*, they petitioned the Lord of Hosts for help in the coming struggle.

Then, a miracle occurred. The wind opposing the Christian fleet switched allegiance; it came completely around and began to blow against the Muslim fleet. Across the galleys of the Holy League, lateen sails were quickly raised just as Ottoman sails were hastily dropped. The sails of the Christian fleet filled as if from a "mighty and confident breath". The Ottoman galley slaves were roused from under their benches and whipped into action.

Throughout the Christian fleet, slaves and convicts who had been chained to their benches were unshackled and handed swords or half pikes. None doubted that a Mighty Providence had intervened on their behalf. They had all been promised freedom in the event of a victory. Favorable winds freed up thousands of Christians for the coming battle. In contrast, each galley slave in the Muslim fleet remained chained to his bench. If his galley went down, he perished with it.

The Christian fleet maintained an extended front of about three miles as it closed on its adversary. On the far right was a squadron of sixty-four galleys commanded by Gian Andrea Doria of Genoa. The center, or main battle commanded by Don John had sixty-three galleys. The ships of his vice admirals were on either side of the *Real*—on the right, the commander of the papal fleet, Antonio Colonna, and, on the left, Sebastian Veniero, the fiery captain-general of the Venetians, who at seventy-six was the oldest man fighting at Lepanto.

The left wing of the Christian line had another sixty-three galleys and was commanded by the Venetian Agostino

Barbarigo. A reserve squadron of thirty-five galleys under the exceptionally brave and competent Marquis of Santa Cruz was centered to the rear of the main battle. The reserve under Santa Cruz would play a critical role in the outcome of the looming engagement.

Ali Pasha was in direct command of the ninety-six warships comprising the Ottoman main battle opposite Don John. He had deployed on his right his best commander, Muhammad Sirrocco, with fifty-six galleys of low draft—their mission was to turn the flank of the Venetian left wing by sailing as close to the shoreline as possible, a place where Venetian galleys with their deeper draft couldn't sail.

On his left, Ali Pasha placed the Algerian Uluch Ali and ninety-three galleys; their mission was to extend the Christian right and try to detach it from the main battle. It was a good plan and might have succeeded were it not for the surprises the Christians had in store for Ali Pasha and his men.

The first surprise was the six heavily armed war galleys (*galleasses)* placed a mile in advance of the Christian line. When Ali Pasha's galleys passed these ungainly but deadly vessels, they came under fire from four hundred harquebusiers, who fired massed volleys into the Janissaries packed on the decks of the Muslim galleys. Then, the fifty-four cannon that were mounted beneath the high decks of each *galleass*, fired broadsides into the Turkish galleys as they attempted to pass the great ships. A single volley destroyed some Ottoman war galleys. A large segment of the advancing crescent was disrupted before it even met the extended battle line of the Christian fleet. It was the very first time that the high-walled *galleasses* with their banks of cannon were ever used in battle. Lepanto signaled the end of oared galleys. Future battles would be decided by broadside cannon and sail and not by infantry assaulting from the decks of oared galleys.

The second surprise in store for Ali Pasha and his fleet was the strange appearance of the Christian war galleys. Don John, on the advice of the Genoese admiral Andrea Doria, had ordered the removal of the iron rams that were mounted on the bows of their galleys. Andrea Doria was a seasoned veteran of galley warfare. He had observed that the ram would not allow the main cannon in the bow to depress at close range—most shots were sent high and harmlessly into the enemies sails and rigging. Without their iron rams, the Christians were able to deliver devastating cannon fire aimed at the water line of the attacking galleys, often sinking them with a single volley.

As the fleets closed for battle, Don John ordered his helmsmen to steer for the enemy's flagship. So, too, did Ali Pasha. Both leaders ignored the convention of galley warfare that flagships did not engage one another. The two flagships collided in a staggering crash, the prow of the larger, heavier *Sultana* smashing its way into the fourth bench of rowers on the *Real*. Grappling lines quickly locked the two ships into a deadly duel.

The third surprise occurred when Ali Pasha and his Janissaries attempted to board the Christian galleys. When the fanatically brave Janissaries began to climb the sides of the *Real*, they reached an unfamiliar, deadly obstacle: all of Don John's galleys had boarding nets stretched from stem to stern. Unable to board, the Janissaries hung in the nets, absorbing the withering fire of the Spanish infantry massed on board the *Real*. Their bravery approached insanity as they tried to grapple their way up the sides of the *Real*, only to be shredded by musketry. More than eight hundred men were now packed shoulder to shoulder on the decks of the two ships, raining arrows and musket balls point-blank into one another. The carnage was terrible. Scores of dead and dying men soon littered both decks.

Then, it was the turn of the Spanish infantry to mount their assault on the *Sultana*. Miguel Cervantes, who fought with distinction at Lepanto, losing the use of his left hand, wrote a passage in *Don Quixote* that describes the great bravery displayed by those who gave their lives boarding an enemy galley:

> The soldier . . . urged on by the honor that nerves him, . . . makes himself a target for all that musketry, and struggles to cross that narrow path to the enemy's ship. And what is still more marvelous, no sooner has one gone down into the depths he will never rise from till the end of the world, then another takes his place; and if he too falls into the sea that waits for him like an enemy, another and another will succeed him without a moment's pause between their deaths; courage and daring the greatest that all the chances of war can show.
>
> (*Don Quixote*, pt I, chap. 38)

Don John's Spanish infantry was forced to muster three times before they gained a foothold on the blood-smeared decks of the *Sultana*. The harquebus (muskets) of the West slowly overcame the traditional composite, recurve bows of the East. Even though the Turkish bowmen might get off as many as thirty arrows before the harquebusier could reload for another shot, the Turkish arrows could not penetrate the armor of the Spanish infantry. The musket balls of the harquebusiers devastated the unarmored Turks, blowing wide swaths through their massed ranks.

Don John was wounded in the final assault on the *Sultana*. Ali Pasha went down with a musket ball to the forehead. An armed convict, one of those freed and armed by Don John, quickly severed Ali's head and hoisted it on a pike. He carried the grisly symbol of victory to the quarterdeck of the *Real*. With their commander visibly dead, the men of the *Sultana* were finally overrun and subdued. Simultaneously, the sacred banner of the Prophet was swept from the masthead and the papal banner raised in its place. A blare of trumpets and cries of "Victory" all down the Christian line signaled Don John's capture of the Muslim flagship.

On the left side of the Christian line, the galleys of the Venetian admiral Agustin Barbarigo remained locked in a desperate struggle. Barbarigo had barely managed to avoid having his line turned by Muhammad Sirrocco. The battle was fearsome. In some instances every man on board a galley was slain or wounded, with "Christian and Muslim lying promiscuously together in the embrace of death" (*Atlantic Monthly*, Dec. 1857, p. 143). Capuchin priests were seen at the front of many boarding parties, leading the assault with an uplifted crucifix. On some Turkish galleys, Christian slaves managed to break their chains and join the battle against their masters.

Slowly, sword in hand, the Christians began to defeat one enemy vessel after another. Admiral Barbarigo was mortally wounded in the struggle, taking an arrow to the eye. Lingering below decks in agony, his officers brought him news that Muhammad Sirrocco had fallen and the enemy was defeated. Giving up his last breath, he exclaimed, "I die contented."

On the right of the Christian line, the superior tactics of Uluch Ali had tricked Andrea Doria. Doria had allowed his fleet to be drawn off the line of battle, opening a gap that allowed the Algerian corsairs to dart through. They immediately began to attack the rear of the Christian main battle. Their initial assault destroyed or captured the galleys of the Maltese fleet.

Uluch Ali might have turned the battle had not the reserve force under Santa Cruz reacted in time to save the day. Yet, it was still a close thing. The reserve galleys descended on the corsairs just as they were boarding the defeated Maltese Knights, all of whom had died defending their galleys at overwhelming odds. In the ensuing struggle, entire galleys had every officer and soldier aboard either killed or dying of their wounds.

Uluch Ali was slowly beaten back by the relentless attack of the reserve galleys led by Santa Cruz. Seeing that the day was lost, he signaled for his remaining thirteen galleys to disengage. They were the only Ottoman forces not killed or captured at Lepanto, and all that remained of the Sultan's once formidable battle fleet.

The Battle of Lepanto lasted until four in the afternoon. As the smoke from the cannon and burning galleys cleared, it became obvious that the Christians had won an astounding victory. Fifteen thousand Christian galley slaves climbed from the filthy benches of the captured Ottoman war galleys, now free men. The Holy League is estimated to have lost only seven thousand men in the battle. Only twelve war galleys were destroyed; a number were badly damaged and had to be sunk. By contrast, the Christian fleet destroyed or captured more than two hundred Ottoman war galleys and nearly one hundred smaller craft.

It was a staggering defeat for the Ottomans—over thirty thousand were slain that afternoon. Untold numbers would later die from their wounds. It is reported that only thirty-five hundred Turkish prisoners were captured out of the one hundred thousand enemy present at the battle. This low number of captives suggests that the Christians gave no quarter to those who attempted to surrender. Thousands were executed when their galleys were captured; thousands more were left to perish in the waves as they attempted to swim to the Aetolian shore. Muslim losses at Lepanto were also staggering in terms of experienced admirals, seamen, and archers. The thirty-four admirals and 120 galley captains who perished, as well as the thousands of trained archers and Janissaries killed in battle, would take years to replace.

It can be argued that Sultan Selim II would have been adding minarets to the Basilica of St. Peter in Rome had the Holy League not prevailed at Lepanto. The Christian fleet, supported by the Rosary and under the remarkable leadership of Don John, delivered Christendom from an Ottoman menace that was certainly poised to sack Rome, with the likelihood of overrunning all of Europe.

The physical and psychological defeat suffered by the Ottomans at Lepanto marked the beginning of the decline of the Ottoman Empire. The Christian victory on that fateful Sunday in October 1571 halted the long advance of Islam against Christendom.

*Pope Pius V and his vision of the Battle of Lepanto.*

# The Aftermath

## By William Cinfici

The significance of the Battle of Lepanto cannot be over-
stated. The defeat of the Ottoman Turkish fleet in 1571 by the
Holy League of the Christians led by Don John of Austria
marked the turning point of Muslim aggression that had made
major attempts to conquer the Christian West. It must be
counted among the most significant battles in history, because
it began the process that ultimately gave us today's map. It can
be said, in a sense, that we are presently in the post-Lepanto
age.

After Lepanto, and especially after the failed Ottoman siege
of Vienna in 1683, the once-mighty Ottoman Empire that
had threatened to overrun the West began a long, slow de-
cline. During this time, it was called "The Sick Man of Eu-
rope", as it began to lose some of its frontier territories. Some
of the nations within it, beginning with Greece in 1829, be-
came independent. The western European powers, namely,
Spain, France, Italy, and the United Kingdom, had taken all
of North Africa from the Turks by the First World War.

After the Turks were defeated in the war, nearly the whole
empire was broken up, leaving only the portion that became
the modern state of Turkey. The remainder of what had been
the Ottoman Empire (the Arabian Peninsula and the Fertile
Crescent) was divided between the United Kingdom and
France, with Saudi Arabia and Iraq being granted indepen-
dence. Ultimately, all the British and French territory would
become the independent Arab states we see on the map of the

Middle East today—all a legacy of the Ottoman defeat at Lepanto.

However, the breakup of the multinational Ottoman Empire has left a legacy of conflict between the peoples who live within its former provinces. A survey of only the current conflicts reveals the problem. It can be argued that eastern Europe, in particular, has undergone a process of de-Ottomanization.

Turkey and its neighbor Greece have teetered on the brink of war numerous times throughout their history over territorial disputes. They have also contested the fate of Cyprus, where tension between the Christian Greek and Turkish Muslim Cypriot communities on the British-held island led to the creation of the Republic of Cyprus in 1960, but later to a rift between the two Cypriot communities, with the Turkish Cypriots occupying the northern third of the island, leaving the remainder de-Ottomanized. Ultimately, Turkey sent troops to the northern part of Cyprus in 1974, where they have remained up to the present, with the situation still unresolved.

In the Balkans, especially in Bosnia and Kosovo, ethnic Slavs and Albanians who had converted to Islam under Ottoman rule have struggled with Christians for control in the aftermath of the breakup of Yugoslavia in the 1990s. There, de-Ottomanization showed an ugly face in the form of "ethnic cleansing", which was inspired by an atheistic Communist leader using nationalism in order to hold onto power while communism was declining virtually everywhere else in Europe. The various Balkan battles, like the conflict over Cyprus, have threatened to embroil Greece and Turkey and a larger war.

Meanwhile, Palestine continues to be one of the greatest sources of conflict between the Islamic world and the West. There, two Palestinian states were granted independence by the British in 1948 out of former Ottoman territory: one Jewish, (Israel); the other, Arab and Muslim (Transjordan, now known as Jordan). Israel, created and defended by the West, is a kind of neo-Crusader state even though it is not Christian. The gates of Jerusalem hold back the onslaught of forces fighting under the banner of the crescent moon.

Sometimes the conflicts that have arisen out of the breakup of the polyglot Ottoman Empire are between fellow Muslims—or even among fellow Arabs. The Kurdish struggle for independence is an example of a conflict between Muslims that arose out of the breakup of the empire. Arabs have fought one another in the war between Iraq and Kuwait.

The destruction of the Ottoman Empire, a process that began at Lepanto, has left another political legacy: an understandable feeling among Muslims of defeat. They find it impossible to accept defeat at the hands of non-Muslims because it is irreconcilable with their belief that Allah supports their cause of making the rest of the world submit (the word "Islam" means "*submission* to the will of Allah"). Indeed, Lepanto must burn like a grain of sand in the eye of Muslim memory. It is worth noting that Muslims, and Arabs, in particular, have long memories. Therefore, the sixteenth century naval battle is part of what historians call the "specious present" for Muslims. In other words, its significance to them is not as a past event, but as an integral part of their present consciousness. It can thus be said that Lepanto has even greater significance for Muslims than for most Westerners.

Unable to defeat the West in conventional battle, militant Muslims have turned to the desperate measure of terrorism, including suicide attacks. The attacks of September 11, 2001, were apparently an attempt to prove that Allah supports them, as well as to recruit new members for the struggle against the West, rather than a serious attempt to militarily or economically defeat the United States, let alone the whole West. Ominously, the attacks have raised the threshold, proving that even bloodier attacks would be necessary in order to achieve their intended purpose, as long as the West remains resolute in its resistance.

Since the fall of the Ottoman Empire, Muslims have focused upon trying to eliminate the state of Israel and upon fighting around the periphery of the Islamic world, as is currently the case from Chechnya to Kashmir, from the Ivory Coast to Indonesia. However, the question now is whether we have reached the point that Hilaire Belloc predicted would come: when Muslims rise again to challenge the West. In *The Great Heresies*, Belloc describes Islam as "the most formidable and persistent enemy which our civilization has had, and may at any moment become as large a menace in the future as it has been in the past" (p. 52). He goes on to make this prediction: "It has always seemed to me possible, and even probable, that there would be a resurrection of Islam and that our sons and grandsons would see the renewal of that tremendous struggle between the Christian culture and what has been for more than a thousand years its greatest opponent" (p. 73).

But in order for Islam to rise, Belloc notes that it needs to unite under a leader: "There is no leader as yet, but enthusiasm might bring one and there are signs enough in the political heavens today of what we may have to expect from the revolt of Islam at some future date—perhaps not far distant" (p. 77).

Although many Muslims do not support military conquest of the West, it is necessary to recognize that a sufficient number of them do, in order to allow for another Sulemein the Magnificent (the great Ottoman Turkish conqueror) to emerge. It is noteworthy that the despots who have emerged in recent years, from the Ayatollah Khomeini to Osama Bin Laden to Saddam Hussein, do appeal to a significant portion of the Arab and Islamic world, despite their brutality even to fellow Muslims, because of their casting of the conflict as one between Islam and West. Although Saddam Hussein's regime was snuffed by overpowering Western forces, led by the United States, the irony remains that the Islamic world still has a better chance of reuniting under one leader than does the Christian West. That is because there is no Christian West.

The great paradox is that although the Christendom prevailed over the Turks at Lepanto and prevented a Muslim takeover of Europe, Christendom subsequently collapsed in Europe, brought down by the forces that were already working against in the sixteenth century: the splintering of Christianity by Protestantism, leading to a loss of faith in general, and the rise of the merchant class over the small independent producer, leading to a loss of freedom and autonomy. It is one thing to force out a boorish dictator, but it is quite another thing to fight a religious war. The West still has the stronger military, but it no longer has the holy men needed to fight a holy war, should it really come to that.

Although the political map changed as a result of the Battle of Lepanto, the greatest legacy of the battle is something that affected the daily lives of millions of Catholics, both across the globe and across the centuries. The feast of Our Lady of the Rosary inspired a more widespread use of this devotional prayer, a prayer that has grown only in significance. It is a prayer that mystifies and even repulses Protestants, and it is a prayer that, ironically, is treated with respect and even sympathy by Muslims, who take devotional prayer quite seriously. While Catholics and Protestants are finding themselves as allies trying to stem the degeneration of the West and may find themselves having to create a new alliance in defense of the West against a new Muslim aggression, they may ultimately have to forge an alliance with the Muslim world against the degeneration of the West. As G. K. Chesterton pointed out, the ultimate purpose of a fight is not to conquer an enemy but to convert him. There is really only one way that is going to happen: prayers are needed for the wind to shift again.

*G. K. Chesterton as he appeared at the time Lepanto was written*

# The Poem

By Dale Ahlquist

The man who was the inspiration for Chesterton's most famous fictional character was also the inspiration for Chesterton's most famous poem. That man was Fr. John O'Connor, the priest who was the model for Father Brown. In the spring of 1911, both Chesterton and Father O'Connor participated in a debate about war. The two friends were apparently on the same side in the debate. Chesterton argued that all wars are religious wars, and Father O'Connor gave a description of the Battle of Lepanto that Chesterton said was "magnificent". It obviously stirred his fertile imagination. Father O'Connor later recalled;

> I told of . . . how Philip the Second of Spain had been assembling his Armada to invade England, and could only spare two ships to face the hundred galleys of the Porte; and how Don John of Austria, the only commander under whom Genoa would agree with Venice, burst the battle-line on a sinking ship, after fighting through all the hours of daylight. And the story of the Pope's prayer all that day, and his vision of the crisis of the action at three in the afternoon, with his vision of the victory about the time of the Angelus. Thus, I take it, came Chesterton to write the incomparable ballad of *Lepanto* (*Father Brown on Chesterton*, p. 85).

Father O'Connor found a scrap of paper that Chesterton used at that event on which he had already jotted down a few lines that were similar to what would later appear in the poem. The battle and its literary possibilities continued to play on Chesterton's mind, as is evident in a *Daily News* column on August 5 of that year. But he actually wrote the poem, interestingly enough, on the 340th anniversary of the battle, October 7, 1911, and it was published that week. According to Father O'Connor, Chesterton finished the poem while the mailman was standing and waiting impatiently for it, "saying he had but ten minutes to get it with his mail to the train" (p. 85). It is amazing to think that this timeless poem was written in the same manner as all of Chesterton's journalistic pieces: in a mad rush under a deadline.

*Lepanto* was first published in *The Eye-Witness* on October 12, 1911. The editor, Hilaire Belloc, recognized the greatness of the poem and would later write that *Lepanto* "is not only the summit of Chesterton's achievement in verse but in all our generation. I have said this so often that I am almost tired of saying it again, but I must continue to say it" (*On the Place of Chesterton*, p. 78).

It is clear that the poem had an immediate and widespread impact on the English-reading public. Less than three years later, in the midst of World War I, Chesterton received a note from John Buchan, saying, "The other day in the trenches we shouted your Lepanto" (Ward, *Gilbert Keith Chesterton*, p. 23).

When Chesterton's official biography appeared in 1943, Maisie Ward called the poem "perhaps his best-known single piece of writing". It was certainly up to that time his most highly praised piece of writing. Maisie Ward claimed that a whole book could be filled with "the tributes it has received" (ibid., p. 371).

But all those tributes, as well as the poem itself, have been forgotten. The neglect, unfortunately, has been deliberate. Though the poem deserves to be studied and appreciated for its literary merits alone, it is purposely avoided in English literature classes. With its steady crescendo that begins with "dim drums throbbing", soon joined by "strong gongs groaning", and continuing to build momentum until it "booms away past Italy", and, finally, bursts "the battle line" with a shout of triumph, this poem is more than just a poem. It is a rousing encounter with history, a pivotal event in history that some people would rather ignore, just as they ignore the poem. *Lepanto* is also an unsettling encounter with Christian history. Though Chesterton is one of the most dearly loved ecumenical writers of modern times, this is not what we would call an ecumenical piece of writing. He does not pull any punches in his criticisms of the Protestants. Though he was not a Catholic when he penned these lines, he clearly defends the Catholic Church. Yet he paints his canvas with the blood of Christian killing Christian, knowing full well that Catholics were as guilty of that kind of slaughter as were Protestants, and paints a Catholic hero, Philip II, almost black. He adds to his palette the "evil hues" of all the disruptive and destructive and divisive ideas that attack or undermine the Church. But just to make things more prickly, he fingers the Prophet Muhammad as the ringleader. So the problem with the poem is that it is a defense of the Catholic Church, of the Crusades, and of war: three things not generally looked kindly upon in today's English literature classes; of course, neither are rhyme and meter. The only twentieth century poetry that is permitted to be studied is that which clashes with everything: with the ear, with history, and with common sense. But there is an irony in that: it is unlikely that any of the professors that actively ignore Chesterton and his poem would even have their jobs if the Battle of Lepanto had gone the other way in 1571. Or if they did have their jobs, they'd all be teaching *One Thousand and One Nights* for probably the one thousand and oneth time.

There is a quality about *Lepanto* that can only be described as nimble. It is a combination of a God-given literary gift and Chesterton's added accomplishment as a craftsman who can make words do what he wants them to. Each stanza seems both carefully constructed and yet utterly spontaneous at the same time. None of the lines sound strained; none of the rhymes are forced. Although most modern poets have given up on rhyme and meter, poetry still wants to rhyme and still wants to sing, and our ears want it to. Chesterton describes rhyme as a kind of homecoming, giving a sense of completeness. Yet very few poets do it very well—Chesterton does. And his marching meter is perfectly suited to this poem. We must also praise Chesterton's dazzling use of alliteration, which adds so much to the beauty and intricacy of almost every line of *Lepanto*:

> Dim drums throbbing, in the hills half heard . . .
> Strong gongs groaning as the guns boom far . . .
> Stiff flags straining . . .
> Then the tuckets, then the trumpets, then the cannons and he comes . . .
> Splashed with a splendid sickness . . .
> They swell in sapphire smoke . . .
> We have set the seal of Solomon . . .
> It is he whose loss is laughter when he counts the wager worth . . .
> He touches, and it tingles, and he trembles . . .
> Thronging of the thousands . . .

The brilliance of Chesterton's *Lepanto* is that in addition to its masterful construction, it takes us inside the story. The poem is presented from the perspectives of several vastly different characters who are somehow connected to the battle. We begin with Sultan Selim II, ("the Soldan of Byzantium"), smirking in his sunny courts in Constantinople, his sneer in the shape of a crescent. He controls the Mediterranean, and the Christian forces have suffered one inglorious defeat after another at his hands. He is poised to take Venice and Rome. The Pope calls for another crusade against the Islamic infidels, but not to try to retake the holy places of Jerusalem. He is trying to defend his own home turf, the seat of Christendom itself: Rome. And he's getting no help. Queen Elizabeth I of England and King Charles IX of France spurn his requests. Germany is worse than useless; it is in open revolt against Rome. King Philip II is loyal to the Pope, but has plans and plots of his own. Venice is certainly aware of the Muslim threat but is also suspicious of the other Christian kingdoms that the Pope is calling on to join the Holy League. And so the Sultan is laughing on the "Golden Horn"; Christendom is divided and weak and is there for the taking.

But off in the distance, half heard, is the sound of drums, and we are introduced to the hero of the poem, Don John of Austria.

The historical Don John of Austria is a perfect Chesterton hero. He is young and brave and charming and confident and devout. He is decisive and speaks with authority. And he swings a sword. His ability not only to command but to command the respect of the diverse and rival soldiers who form the Holy League is an astonishing achievement—almost as much as winning the battle itself. Add to that his medieval sense of chivalry, and a pet lion cub, to boot. Chesterton could not have invented a more romantic character. It is perfectly correct to portray Don John as the one last noble knight in Europe ready to lead one last crusade.

Chesterton calls him a troubadour, just as he calls all his heroes troubadours. St. Francis of Assisi is a troubadour. The Pickwickians are troubadours. Robert Browning is a troubadour. Gabriel Syme is a troubadour. A troubadour is a romantic, someone who is inspired, someone who lives out his art, someone who *is* a poem.

Don John begins his ride to the sea, and the rhythm of the poem reflects the marching of soldiers and the beating of drums, even the flourish of trumpets and the excitement of preparing for a great battle.

Next we meet Muhammad ("Mahound"), who from his comfortable perch in paradise hears those distant drums. But just as he is introduced, Chesterton begins to interweave the action of the poem. When a stanza begins with the presentation of a new character, the second line, in parentheses, describes the progress of Don John on the way to the battle and throughout the battle itself.

Chesterton grants Muhammad, the founder of the Islamic religion, the very paradise the Prophet promised, but it is not heaven. Heaven is contentment, and the Prophet is anything but content. In spite of the luxurious surroundings and the ready nymphs, the Prophet knows a threat when he hears one. It is the familiar sound of a crusade. It is "the voice that shook our palaces—four hundred years ago" (l. 63).

In the poem, Muhammad's contempt for Christianity is explicit. He calls upon all the forces of hell that are at his disposal to fight the Christian menace. Chesterton gives a vivid description of evil spirits, swelling "in sapphire smoke out of the blue cracks of the ground" (l. 54). And he gives a concise description of hell, as a place "where fallen skies and evil hues and eyeless creatures be" (l. 51). "Fallen skies" is a reference to spiritual pride, in particular to Lucifer, who fell from heaven and whose new domain is a mockery of heaven, just as the sea mocks the sky. Satan, Chesterton said, fell by the force of gravity, and he sinks as low as he can go. "Evil hues" refer to the contrast between the lively and bold Christian colors to their pale and sickly hues, which are merely their shadows or reflections, or the colors after the colors have run out of them, after the blood and life has run out of them. For example, the shield of St. George combines red and white together. They have been joined by a cross, but the red is still red and the white is still white; they have not melted together into pink. And in Christianity, the strong, contrasting ideas of love and wrath have not melted together into some vague, indistinct, wishy-washy philosophy. Christianity, as Chesterton says, has always had a healthy hatred of pink. And "eyeless creatures" is a reference to wandering in spiritual darkness. Where there is no vision the people perish. Hell is a place where there is no vision; it is a place of darkness. One of the reasons we are afraid of hell is that we are afraid of the dark. We are afraid of the dark, Chesterton says, because it represents "a blinding agnosticism". It's not just fear; it's terror. "Fear is of the body, perhaps; but terror is only of the soul" (*Lunacy and Letters*, p. 157).

It is a spiritual battle, and Muhammad knows it. He begins at once to command his army of demons to fight the saints. You can defeat the Christians by taking away their most powerful warriors: the saints. Destroy the relics. Destroy that fundamental part of the culture. Destroy the very mountains if you have to in order to destroy the hermits' caves, because every cave is incubating a saint. It worked once before. The hermits were the soul of Eastern Christianity. They were like sentinels, lonely outposts in the desert, doing what even the disciples themselves could not do: staying awake, watching, and praying. Ironically, it was a hermit who led the very first, short-lived Crusade. But when the hermits were gone, so was Eastern Christianity. It fell not with the fall of Constantinople, but with the loss of the hermits.

It is a spiritual battle, but Muhammad also knows that the grave danger to Islam from Christianity is something quite physical—not just the physical battle on the sea between ships and sabers, but something more supremely physical: the Incarnation. As Chesterton says of Christianity, "its very soul is a body" (*Short History of England, CW* 20:441).

Muhammad rallies his troops with grand claims about the superiority of Islam. *We* have the wisdom of Solomon. *We* have all the knowledge. *We* have all the truth. And we have to crush the pretenders and idolaters who dare attack Islam.

But Don John continues his relentless march to the sea.

After Muhammad, we meet Muhammad's counterpart: St. Michael. Like the Prophet, the archangel also surveys the situation from a high place ("on his Mountain", l. 74). He, too, recognizes another crucial battle coming, the kind he has fought before, and he is compelled again to gather the faithful and join the fight. But he has none of Muhammad's success in putting an army together. When he shakes his lance and calls the Christian troops to march out of the North and join Don John, his battle cry goes unheeded. The North is in disarray. In fact, it is also destroying relics and killing monks, not in the name of Allah, but in the name of Christ. Things are "tangled" (l. 80) indeed when "Christian killeth Christian" (l. 82).

Long after this poem was written, and after his conversion, Chesterton visited Rome and reflected again on the events of the second half of the sixteenth century, the beginning of "the last agony of Christendom", when Christian Europe was facing its greatest peril from without, with the Muslim threat in the Mediterranean, and was also being splintered from within by the Protestant rebellion. "The Reformation has been called many things, good and bad," he wrote, "and there was certainly much in it both defensible and indefensible. But that is the thing about it which I for one find it hardest to forgive. It was a Christian mutiny during a Moslem invasion" (*The Resurrection of Rome, CW* 21:349–50).

And lest the Catholics start feeling smug, or even too comfortable with the poem, the next character who steps onto the stage is King Philip II of Spain, Don John's half brother. While most sincere Catholics consider Philip a hero of the Counter-Reformation, a devout and determined defender of the faith, G. K. Chesterton, whom they regard in the same way, portrays Philip as a paranoid, reclusive, diseased and murderous coward. And did we say "jealous"? Even the most sympathetic historians detect a "whiff" of envy. The record is pretty clear that Philip made Don John's life miserable afterward—just how miserable is a matter for debate. There is nothing like a little court intrigue to make things, well, intriguing. At any rate, he's what Don John has waiting for him, should he survive the Turkish fleet.

But Don John *"is armed upon the deck"* (l. 93) and ready to face the enemy.

Then we have a brief appearance by the Pope, praying in his chapel and miraculously seeing the battle far away—a distinct contrast from the eyeless creatures of a few stanzas earlier. The picture that the Pope sees is the picture Chesterton shows us: the enemies facing off. The Turkish galleys are lined up in the shape of the Muslim crescent; the Holy League is in the shape of the Christian cross. It is another case of the real thing being so poetic that it could not possibly have been made any better by Chesterton's pen. It is also a case of the symbol and the reality being the same thing: the Cross literally doing battle with the Crescent.

Then we get another vision of hell. Not evil spirits this time, but "Christian captives sick and sunless" (l. 118), chained to their oars in the galleys of "brown, black-bearded chiefs" (l. 116). It is a moving image of the unimaginable: the suffering shared by slaves throughout the centuries who have been tortured mercilessly by heartless tyrants.

And just when hope seems totally spent, Don John *"has burst the battle-line"* (l. 127), Chesterton using the very phrase he heard from Father O'Connor. Christ-like, Don John has set the captives free. The battle is won for Christendom.

Finally, almost as an afterthought after the climax of the action as Don John rides home victorious at the end of the poem, one more historical character is introduced. A soldier who was really there, who really fought and really was wounded, and who would return to his native Spain to create one of the greatest pieces of literature of all time: Cervantes. Chesterton has him already envisioning Don Quixote as the Battle of Lepanto concludes: the fictional knight-errant, riding in vain, in contrast to the last true knight who fought the last battle of the last Crusade.

The poem begins and ends with a smile. The first is the smile of the Sultan before the battle. He is relishing his dominance of the Mediterranean and the fact that he has the Christian West on its heels. The second smile is that of Cervantes, at the end of the battle when the Sultan's forces have been defeated. His is a smile of relief at the victory, but also one that is already looking forward to the comical adventures of the "lean and foolish knight" Don Quixote. The difference between the smiles signifies the difference between East and West, between Muslim and Christian, between a Sultan and a soldier, between a tyrant and an artist. The Sultan presumes victory but then is stunned by defeat; the writer is surprised by victory and then invents a perpetually defeated knight who "forever rides in vain" (l. 141).

The Sultan and the writer both smile. Cervantes, however, smiles "not as Sultans smile" because the Sultan's smile is a sneer, and the writer's smile is a laugh, which for Chesterton sums up the whole difference between fate and free will. Chesterton, the jolly journalist, is never far from laughter.

Chesterton was often asked to recite his poems, but he seldom complied with the request, preferring instead to recite other people's poems. It not only has to do with his humility, but it seems that Chesterton could remember the things he read, but not the things he had written. Once he had written them, he had no more use for them. There is only one documented instance of him reciting *Lepanto*. It was not for a large audience, or even for a gathering of friends. It was for one small boy who was visiting Chesterton's home one afternoon. He was only eight or nine years old. Many years later, recalling that special day, he said that he probably did not understand very much of the poem, "but the fact that mine was the ear he had chosen, as much as the flashing and reverberating words of *Lepanto* itself, impressed and excited me" (Nicolas Bentley, quoted in, Ward, *Return to Chesterton*, 110).

G. K. Chesterton has been called a master without a masterpiece. As a criticism it has the strength of keeping Chesterton's works out of the classroom and keeping him relegated to a footnote in textbooks, but it has the weakness of not meaning anything. Masters create masterpieces, and Chesterton created several. I would argue that when it comes to the essay form, Chesterton created thousands of masterpieces. And his *Father Brown* collection is uniformly praised as a masterpiece of detective fiction. And as an example of sheer rhetoric and sustained argument, there is not a book in the twentieth century that surpasses *Orthodoxy*. But even if we took all those away, Chesterton deserves to be placed among the immortals of literature for this poem alone. Like every masterpiece, it is a work of art that continues to get better and better with time and leaves the reader in awe. It should be memorized and studied and discussed and revisited by every student of English poetry and world history. It should be in every anthology of English literature and part of the standard syllabus in every class of English 101—but it isn't. Hardly anyone knows of the poem. It suffers in obscurity because of a combined prejudice against rhyme and meter, against Catholicism, and against G. K. Chesterton.

But we hope that it will be discovered and appreciated by a new generation. As for this generation that continues to neglect the poem, we can only repeat—charitably, of course—the words of Hilaire Belloc: "People who cannot see the value of *Lepanto* are half dead. Let them remain so" (*On the Place of Chesterton*, p. 78).

*Two Essays*
*by G. K. Chesterton*

# The True Romance

## By G. K. Chesterton

This is a perfectly true story; but there is in it a certain noble irony, not very easy to analyse, which goes down to the very roots of Christianity.

Some hundreds of years ago there was born in one of the southern peninsulas of Europe a man whose life was very like the life of a boy in one of Mr. Henty's books. He did everything that could possibly be expected of a boy's hero; he ran away to sea; he was trusted by admirals with important documents; he was captured by pirates; he was sold as a slave. Even then he did not forget the duties of a Henty hero. He made several picturesque and desperate attempts at escape, scaling Moorish walls and clambering through Moorish windows. He confronted the considerable probability of torture, and defied it. But he was not like the unscrupulous prison-breakers, like Cellini or Casanova, ready to break the world as well as the wall, or his promise as well as his prison. He remembered that he was the hero of an honest boy's storybook, and behaved accordingly. Long afterwards his country collected the depositions of the other Christian captives, and they were an astonishing chorus. They spoke of this man as if he were a sort of saint, of the almost unearthly unselfishness with which he divided their distresses and defied their tormentors. As one reads the coldest biographical account one can feel the alien air, that enormous outside world of Asia and Africa that has always felt slavery to be a natural and even monotonous thing. One feels the sunny silence of great open courts, with fountains in the midst, guarded here and there by mute, white-clad, unnatural men; dim and secret divans smelling of smoke and sweet stuff; grass burnt out of the bare ground, and palm trees prised like parasols. And in all this still horror of heat and sleep, the one unconquered European still leaping at every outlet of adventure or escape; climbing a wall as he might a Christian apple tree, or calling for his rights as he might in a Christian inn.

Nor did our hero miss that other great essential of the schoolboy protagonist; which is accidental and even improbable presence on a tremendous historical occasion. All who love boys' books as they should be loved know that Harry Harkaway, as well as crossing cutlasses with an individual smuggler or slaver, must also manage to be present at the Battle of Trafalgar. The young musketeer from Gascony, however engrossed by duels with masked bravos or love letters to Marguerite de Valois, must not forget to put in an appearance at the Massacre of St. Bartholomew. Here also my hero in real life equaled any of the heroes of juvenile fiction; for he was present and took an active part in one of the most enormous and earth-changing events in history. Europe, in the age in which he lived, was, as it is now, in one of its recurring periods of division and disease. The Northern nations were full of sombre fanaticisms; the Southern nations of equally sombre statecraft and secrecy. The country of the man I describe was indeed rich in territory; but its King was morbid, mean, and lethargic; a man of stagnant mysteries, as he looks in those fishy, pasty-faced portraits which still endure. His strong but sinister imperial armies were engaged in wars, more or less unjust on both sides, with the sinister enthusiasms of the North; the whole civilization was bitter and trivial, and apparently tumbling to pieces. And at this moment appeared upon its Eastern borders its ancient and awful enemy, the Turk.

Like genii summoned out of that Eastern sea by the seal of Solomon, robed in the purple of the twilight or the green of the deep, rose the tall, strange, silent sails of the admirals of Islam. The very shapes of the ships on the horizon were unfamiliar and fearful; and when they came close to the Greek islands, prow and stern showed the featureless ornament of the foes of idolatry; that featureless ornament in which one seems to see a hundred faces, as one does in a Turkey carpet. The ships came silently and ceaselessly, in numbers that, it seemed, had never been seen since Xerxes seemed stronger than the gods. And every hermit on a Greek headland, or little garrison of knights upon an islet in the Mediterranean, looked at them and saw the sunset of Christendom.

They encircled and besieged a stronghold in that central sea, whose fall would have been the fall of Europe. In the general paralysis the Pope, with one exception, was the only man who moved promptly; he put out the Papal galleys and addressed a public prayer for help to all the Christian princes. The cold and sluggish King doubted and hung back, just as he would have done in the historical novel. But he had a half-brother—as he would have had in the novel. The half-brother was every bit as brave, handsome, brilliant, and generous as he would have been in the novel. The King was as jealous of him as he would have been in the novel. This quite genuine hero rushed to the rescue, and in such crises it is popularity that tells, even in empires. The young Prince had already won romantic victories in Africa, but he could bring only a few ships in time for the attack. Then was waged on that blue and tideless sea what must have been one of the most splendid and appalling battles that ever stained the sea or smoked to the sun. The Turks slew eight thousand Christian soldiers, and the sea drank galley after galley of the Christian fleet. But the fight was sustained with that terrible and intolerant patience that only comes in a collision of strong creeds, when one whole cosmos really crashes into the other. Before night the tide of that river of blood began to turn. Thirty thousand of the Turks were killed or taken prisoners, and out of the Turkish ports and galleys came into light and liberty twelve thousand European slaves.

This was the great battle of Lepanto, and of course our hero was there, sword in hand; of course he was wounded there. I can fancy him standing on the deck, with his arm in a sling and looking at the slender escape of Europe and the purple wreck of Asia with a sad, crooked smile on his face. For he was a person whose face was capable of expressing both pity and amusement. His name was Miguel de Cervantes Saavedra, commonly called Cervantes. And having another arm left, he went home and wrote a book called *Don Quixote*, in which he ridiculed romance and pointed out the grave improbability of people having any adventures.

Originally from *Daily News*, August 5, 1911
Reprinted in *A Handful of Authors*

# If Don John of Austria Had Married Mary Queen of Scots

## By G. K. Chesterton

Why is it that the world's most famous love story, after the archetypal story of Adam and Eve, is the story of Antony and Cleopatra? I for one should answer, to begin with, because of the solid truth of the story of Adam and Eve. I have often wondered whether, when the moderns have done playing with that story, burlesquing it, and turning it upside down and tacking on a modern moral like a new tail, or expanding it into an evolutionary fantasia that nobody can make head or tail of, it will ever occur to anybody to see how sensible it is, exactly as it stands. Even if it is an old fable, the old fable is much truer with the old moral. Christians are not constrained, and least of all Christians of my own confession, to treat Genesis with the heavy verbalism of the Puritan—the Hebraiser who knows no Hebrew. But the curious thing is that the more literally we take it the truer it is; and even if it were materialised and modernised into a story of Mr. and Mrs. Jones, the old moral would still be the sound one. A man naked and with nothing of his own is given by a friend the free run of all the fruits and flowers of a very beautiful estate; and only asked to promise that he will not interfere with one particular fruit-tree. If we all talk till we are as old as Methuselah, the moral remains the same for any honourable man. If he breaks his word he is a cad; if he says, "I broke my word because I believe in breaking all limitations and expanding into infinite progress and evolution," he is ten times more of a cad; and has, moreover, become a bore as well as a bounder. But it is this modern suggestion, that Man was right to be bored with Eden and to demand evolution (otherwise mere change), that is very relevant to the question I have asked about Antony and Cleopatra. It is also very relevant to the question I am going to ask about two other famous figures in history, a woman and a man.

For upon this modern theory the Fall really was the Fall; for it was the first action that had only tedium as a motive. Progress began in boredom; and, heaven knows, it sometimes seems likely to end in it. And no wonder; for of all utter falsehoods the most false, I think, is this notion that men can be happy in movement, when nothing but dullness drives them on from behind. Children, and such happy people, can go on from something they really like to something they will like more. But if ever there was a whisper that might truly come from the devil, it is the suggestion that men can despise the beautiful things they have got, and only delight in getting new things because they have not got them. It is obvious that, on that principle, Adam will tire of the tree just as he has tired of the garden. "It is enough that there is always a beyond"; that is, there is always something else to get tired of. All progress based on that mood is truly a Fall; man did fall, does fall, and we can today see him falling. It is the great progressive proposition; that he must seek only for enjoyment because he has lost the power to enjoy. Now this shadow of failure on all fame and civilisation which the agnostic poet preferred to call "the something that infects the world," and I shall cause general pain by calling Original Sin, does manifest itself markedly in the sort of historical legends that exist. But I would urge here that it appears in the historical legends that do not exist. I refer especially to that grand historical episode of the heroic honeymoon, otherwise called the marriage of pure minds, which I study here as closely as is possible in a case that does not exist. It is a remarkable fact, when we consider how much happiness love has doubtless given to mankind as a whole, that mankind has never pointed to any great historical example of a hero and a heroine wedded in a way entirely worthy of them; of a great man and a great woman united by a great love that was entirely supreme and satisfying, as in the tradition of the gigantic loves of Eden. Anybody who imagines that I am talking pessimism, about ordinary people in love, will impute to me the very reverse of what I mean. Millions of people have been happy in love and marriage, in the ordinary way of human happiness; but then that precisely consists in a certain commonsense admission of original sin; in humility and pardon and taking things as they come. But there has not been any example on the grand scale, of a perfect marriage—that has remained in human memory like a great monument. All those monuments, though often of the purest marble, hewn from the loftiest mountain, have very clearly across them the crack from the earthquake in the beginning. The noblest knight of the Middle Ages, St. Louis, was less happy in his marriage than in all other relations. Dante did not marry Beatrice; he lost his love in infancy and found her again in Paradise or in a dream. Nelson was a great lover, but we cannot say that his love made him more great, since it made him do in Naples the only mean action of his life. These historic examples have become legends or traditions; but they have become tragic traditions. And the central literary tradition of all is that typically tragic one I have named, in which even perfect love was whimsically imperfect, and certainly suffered by very imperfect people; in which the hero learned no lesson except delay; in which the heroine inspired nothing except defeat; in which romance made him less than a Caesar and has unkindly compared her to a snake; in which the man was weakened by love and the woman by lovers. Men have taken Antony and Cleopatra as the perfect love story, precisely because it is the imperfect love story. It mirrors the thwarting, the unworthiness, the disproportion which they have felt as spoiling so many splendid passions and divine desires; and mirrors them all the more truly because the mirror is cracked. I imagine that poets will never leave off writing about Antony and Cleopatra; and all they write will be in the mood of that great French poet of our own time, who describes the Roman warrior gazing into the unfathomable eyes of the Egyptian queen, and seeing beneath a spinning and sparkling light the eddies of a vast sea, filled with the rout of all his ships.

I have here dared to call up out of the dust another warrior, whose destiny turned also with the topsails and high poops of the galleys; and another woman, whose legend also has been sometimes twisted into the legend of a snake. There was never any doubt about the beautiful colours or graceful curves of the snake; but, in fact, the woman was not a snake, but very much of a woman; even by the account of those who call her a wicked woman. And the man was not only a warrior, but a conqueror; and his great ships sweep through history not merely to defeat, but to a high deliverance, in which he did not lose the empire, but saved the world. Whatever else we may think of the woman, none can doubt where her heart would have been in that battle, or what sort of song of praise she would have sent up after that victory. There was much about her that was militant, though her life might well have sickened her of militancy; there was much about him that was sensitive and sympathetic with that wider world of culture for which her soul sickened till she died. They were made for each other; they were in fact the heroic lovers, or perfect human pair, for whom we have looked elsewhere in history in vain. There was only one small defect in their purple and impassioned love story; and that is that they never met.

In truth, this dream began to drift through my mind when I first read a parenthetical remark by Andrew Lang, in a historical study about Philip of Spain. Referring to the King's half-brother, the famous Don John of Austria, Lang remarked casually: "He intended to carry off Mary Queen of Scots," and added caustically: "He was incapable of fear." Of course nobody is incapable of fear. He was certainly, in the common sense, incapable of *obeying* fear: but, if I understand the type, he was not incapable of *enjoying* fear as an element in a mystery like that of love. It is exactly because love has lost that slight touch of fear, that it has become in our time so flat and flippant and vulgar; when it has not become laboriously biological, not to say bestial. And Mary was dangerous as well as in danger; that heart-shaped face looking out of the ruff in so many pictures was like a magnet, a talisman, a terrible jewel. There was, even then, in the idea of eloping with the tragic yet attractive Franco-Scottish princess, all the ancient savour of the romances about delivering a lady from dragons, or even disenchanting her out of the shape of a dragon. But though the idea was romantic, it was also in a sense what is now called psychological; for it exactly answered the personal needs of two very extraordinary personalities.

If ever there was a man who ought to have rounded off his victorious career by capturing something more human and spiritual and satisfying than wreaths of laurel or flags of defeated foes, it was Don John of Austria. Because his actual historical life rises on a wave of conquest in relation to these things, and then sinks again into something less epical and simple, his life has something of the appearance of an anticlimax; and reads like a mere stale maxim that all victories are vanities. He tried to crown his chief exploit by founding a kingdom of his own, and was prevented by the jealousy of his brother; he then went, somewhat wearily, I imagine, as the representative of the same brother to the Flemish fields laid waste by the wars of the Dutch and the Duke of Alva. He set out to be more merciful and magnanimous than the Duke of Alva; but he died in a net or tangle of policies; of which the only touch of poetry was a suggestion of poison.

But in that broad and golden dawn of the Renaissance, full of classical legends, carrying off Mary Stuart would have been like carrying off Helen of Troy. In that red sunset of the old chivalric romance (for the sunrise and the sunset were both in that bewildering sky) it would have seemed a magnificent materialisation of one of those strange and stately public love affairs, or knightly services, which preserved something of the Courts of Love and the pageant of the Troubadours; as when Rudel publicly pledged himself to an unknown lady in a castle in the east, almost as distant as a castle east of the sun; or the sword of Bayard sent across the mountains its remote salute to Lucretia. That one of these great loves of the great should actually be achieved in the grand style, that, I fancy, would have been a wildly popular episode in that epoch. And to the career of Don John it would have given a climax and a clue of meaning which its merely military successes could not give; and handed his name down in history and (what is much more important) in legend and literature, as a happier Antony married to a nobler Cleopatra. And when he looked into her eyes he would not have seen only bright chaos and the catastrophe of Actium, the ruin of his ships and his hopes of an imperial throne; but rather the flying curve and crescent of the Christian ships, sweeping to the rescue of the Christian captives, and blazed upon their golden sails the sunburst of Lepanto.

The converse is also true. If ever there was a woman who was manifestly meant, destined, created, and as it were crying aloud to be carried off by Don John of Austria, or some such person, it was Mary Queen of Scots. If ever there was a woman who went to seed for want of meeting any sort of man who was anything like her equal, it was she. The tragedy of her life was not that she was abnormal, but that she was normal. It was the crowd all round her that was abnormal. There is almost a sort of antic allegory, in that sense, in such accidents as the fact that Rizzio had a hump and Bothwell some sort of a squint. If her story seems now to be steeped in morbidity, it was because the mob was morbid.

Unfortunately for this illfated queen, she was not morbid. It is the other characters, each in his own way, which pass before us in misshapen outlines like the dwarfs and lunatics in some tropic tragedy of Ford or Webster, dancing round a deserted queen. And, by a final touch, all these ungainly figures seem more tolerable than the one that is externally elegant, the hollow doll, Darnley; just as a handsome waxwork can seem more uncanny than an ugly man. In that sense she had seen handsome men and ugly men and strong men and clever men; but they were all half-men; like the hideous cripples imagined by Flaubert, living in their half-houses with their half-wives and half-children. She never met a complete man; and Don John was very complete. In that sense she had been given many things; the crown of Scotland, the prospect of the crown of France; the prospect of the crown of England. She had been given everything except fresh air and the sunlight treatment; and all that is typified by the great ships with their golden castles and their leaping flags, that go forth to meet the winds of the world.

We know why Mary Stuart was killed. She was not killed for having killed her husband, even if she had killed her husband; and recent study of the Casket Letters suggests that her enemies are more clearly convicted of forgery than she was ever convicted of murder. She was not killed for trying to kill Elizabeth, even if the whole story of trying to kill Elizabeth was not a fiction employed by those who were trying to kill Mary. She was not killed for being beautiful. That is one of the many popular slanders on poor Elizabeth. She was killed for being in good health.

Perhaps she was the only person who was ever condemned and executed merely for being in good health. The legend which represented Elizabeth as a lioness and Mary as a sort of sickly snake is largely abandoned; anyhow, it is the very reverse of the fact. Mary was very vigorous; a strong rider, and as a dancer almost ready to outrun the Modern Girl. Curiously enough, her contemporary portraits do not convey much of her charm, but do convey a great deal of her vigour. But, as anyone may have noticed in the animal spirits of some of the finest actresses, vigour has sometimes a great deal to do with charm. Now it was essential to the policy of Cecil, and the oligarchs rich with the loot of the old religion, that Mary should die for Elizabeth, and Mary, despite her misfortunes, did not show the smallest disposition to die. Elizabeth, on the other hand, was still dying rather than still living. And when the Catholic heir inherited, it might go ill with the Protestant lords. They therefore applied to Mary, at Fotheringay, one of the sharpest possible remedies for good health, which has seldom been known to fail.

Her energy, which had thus brought her to her death, had also brought her through her life; and may be the key to many of the riddles of her life. It may be that her repeated ill-luck in marriage embittered her more than it might a woman less normal and elemental; and that the very levities, which led to her being painted as a harlot or a vampire, sprang from her primary fitness to be a mother and a wife. It may be (for all I know) that a fairly healthy person, in such a horrible experience, might have wasted her natural instincts on some violent adventurer like Bothwell; those things are always possible; but I confess I could never see that in this case they were necessary. I have often fancied that the alliance may have been more politic, and even cynical, than appeared to that fine romantic novelist, the forger of the Casket Letters. Or it might have been surrender to a sort of blackmail; it might have been many things. Anyhow, being surrounded by brutes, she chose the best brute; though he is always represented as the worst. He was the only one of them who was a man as well as a brute; and a Scotsman as well as a man. He at least never betrayed her to Elizabeth; and all the others did nothing else. He kept the borders of her kingdom against the English like a good subject and a normal soldier; and she might very well have thrown herself under his protection for that alone. But whether or not she sought satisfaction in such a marriage, I am sure that she never found satisfaction in it; I am sure she found only a new phase of the long degradation of living with her inferiors.

There was always in her heart a hunger for civilisation. It is an appetite not easily appreciated now, when people are so over-civilised that they can only have a hunger for barbarism. But she loved culture as the Italian artists of the previous century had loved it; as something not only beautiful but bright and shining and new; like Leonardo's first sketches of flying-machines or the full revelations of perspective and light. She was the Renaissance chained up like a prisoner; just as Don John was the Renaissance roaming the world like a pirate. This was, of course, the perfectly simple explanation of her frequent and friendly toleration of a hunchback like Rizzio and a young lunatic like Chastelard. They were Italy and France; they were music and letters; they were singing-birds from the South who had happened to perch on her window-sill. If there are still any historians who suppose that they were anything more to her than that, especially in the case of the Italian secretary, I can only say that such learned old gentlemen must be pretty much on the moral and mental level of Darnley and his company of cut-throats. Even if she was a wicked woman, there is no sense in supposing that she was not an intelligent woman, or that she never wished to turn from her laborious and life-long wickedness for a little intelligent conversation. The apology for my own (somewhat belated) experiment in matchmaking is that she might have been very different, when married to a man who was quite as brave as Bothwell and quite as intelligent as Rizzio, and, in a more practical and useful fashion, at least as romantic as Chastelard.

But we must not be romantic; that is, we must not concern ourselves with the real feelings of real and recognisable human beings. It is not allowed. We must now sternly turn our attention to scientific history; that is, to certain abstractions which have been labelled The Elizabethan Settlement, the Union, the Reformation, and the Modern World. I will leave the Romantics, those unpresentable Bohemians (with whom, of course, I would not be seen for worlds), to decide at what date and crisis they would like Don John finally to fulfil his design; whether his shining ship is to appear in the wide waters of the Forth as the mad mob in Edinburgh is waving scurrilous scrolls and banners before the window of the Queen; or, on the contrary, a dark boat with a solitary figure is to slide across the glassy stillness of Loch Leven; or a courier hot with haste in advance of a new army hurl a new challenge into the bickering parleys of Carberry, or a herald emblazoned with God knows what eagles and castles and lions (and presumably a bar sinister) blow a trumpet before the barred portals of Fotheringay. I leave that to them; they know all about it. I am an earnest and plodding student of the dry scientific details of history; and we really must consider the possible effect on such details as England,

Scotland, Spain, Europe, and the world. We must suppose, for the sake of argument, that Don John was at least sufficiently strong to assert Mary's claim to sovereignty in Scotland to begin with; and, despite the unpleasant moralising of the mob in Edinburgh, I think such a restoration would have been generally successful in Scotland. Professor Phillimore used to say that the tragedy of Scotland was that she had the Reformation without the Renaissance. And I certainly think that, while Mary and the southern prince were discussing Plato and Pico della Mirandola, John Knox would have found himself a little out of his depth. But on the assumption of popular rulers and a strong Spanish backing, which is the essence of this fantasy, I should say that a people like the Scots would have gobbled up the strong meat of the Revival of Learning quicker than anybody else. But in any case, there is another point to be considered. If the Scots did not figure prominently in the Renaissance, they had, in their own way, figured most brilliantly in the Middle Ages. Glasgow was one of the oldest universities; Bruce was counted the fourth knight in Christendom; and Scotland, not England, continued the tradition of Chaucer. The chivalrous side of the regime would surely have awakened noble memories, even in that ignoble squabble. I must here unfortunately omit a very fine chapter from the unpublished Romance, in which the lovers ride down to Melrose (if necessary by moonlight) to the reputed resting-place of the Heart of Bruce; and recall (in ringing phrases) how Spanish and Scottish spears had once charged side by side upon the Saracen, and hurled far ahead, like a bolt above the battle, the heart of a Scottish King. This fine piece of prose must not delay us, however, from facing the next fact; which is that Mary, once safe, would survive as the Queen of England as well as Scotland. It is enough to say that medieval memories might have awakened in the North; and the Scots might even have remembered the meaning of

Holyrood. Don John died trying to keep his temper with Dutch Calvinists, about ten years before the affair of the Armada; and, much as I admire him, I am glad he did. I do not want my individual dream or romance, about the rescue and elopement of Mary Stuart, mixed up with that famous international collision, in which as an Englishman I am bound to sympathise with England and as an Anti-Imperialist with the smaller nation. But, it may be said, how can an Englishman in any case reconcile himself to a romance that would involve the Elizabethan policy being overthrown by a Spanish prince, the throne occupied by a Scottish queen; or some part at least of the Armada's purposes achieved? To which I answer that such a question recoils ruinously on those who ask it. Let them merely compare what might have happened with what did happen. Was Mary a Scot? We endured one in her son. Was Don John a foreigner? We submitted to one when we expelled the grandson of her son. Mary was as English as James the First. Don John was as English as George the First. The fact is that, whatever else our policy of insular religion (or whatever we call it) may have done, it certainly did not save us from alien immigration, or even from alien invasion. Some may say we could not accept a Spaniard, when we had been recently fighting the Spaniards. But, when we did accept a Dutch prince, we had been recently fighting the Dutch. Blake as well as Drake might complain that his victories had been reversed; and that we had, after all, allowed the broom of Van Tromp to sweep not only the English seas, but the English land. A whole generation before the first George came from Hanover, William of Orange had marched across England with an invading army from Holland. If Don John had really brought an Armada with him (and Armadas are often awkward during elopements) he could hardly have inflicted a heavier humiliation on us than that. But, of course, the truth is that I am sensitive on the point of patriotism;

much more sensitive than anybody was in those days. Extreme nationalism is a relatively new religion; and what these people were thinking of was the old sort of religion. It really made a great difference to them that Dutch William was a Calvinist while Don John was a Catholic; and that whatever George the First was (and he was nearly nothing) he was not a Papist. That brings me to a much more vital phase of my vision of what never happened. But those who expect me to break forth into thunders of theological anathema, will here be rather abruptly disappointed.

I have no intention, I have no need, to argue here about Luther and Leo and the rights and wrongs of the revolt of new sects in the North. I need not do so, for the simple reason that I do not believe, in the case here imagined, that we should have been primarily concerned about the North. I believe we should have realised instead the enormously important position in the South; and even more so in the East. All eyes would have been turned to a far more central battle of civilisation; and the hero of that battle was Don John of Austria.

It has been remarked, and not untruly, that the Papacy seemed curiously negligent of the northern danger from Protestantism. It was; but chiefly because it was not at all negligent of the eastern danger from Islam. Throughout all that period Pope after Pope issued appeal after appeal to the princes of Europe to combine in defence of all Christendom against the Asiatic attack. They had hardly any response; and only a scratch fleet of their own galleys with some Venetian, Genoese, and others, could be sent to stop the Turk from sweeping the whole Mediterranean. This is the huge historic fact which the northern doctrinal quarrels have concealed; and that is why I am not concerned here with the northern doctrinal quarrels. That age was not the age of the Reformation. It was the age of the last great Asiatic invasion, which very nearly destroyed Europe. About the time the Reformation was beginning, the Turks, in the very middle of Europe, destroyed at a blow the ancient kingdom of Bohemia. About the time the Reformation had finished its work, the hordes out of Asia were besieging Vienna. They were foiled by the stroke of Sobieski the Pole, as a hundred years before by the stroke of Don John of Austria. But they came as near as that to submerging the cities of Europe. It must also be remembered that this last Moslem thrust was really a savage and incalculable thing, compared with the first thrust of Saladin and the Saracens. The high Arab culture of the Crusades had long perished; and the invaders were Tartars and Turks and a rabble from really barbarous lands. It was not the Moors but the Huns. It was not Saladin against Richard or Averroes against Aquinas; it was something much more like the worst and wildest shocker about the Yellow Peril.

I have a great respect for the real virtues and the sane if sleeping virility of Islam. I like that element in it that is at once democratic and dignified; I sympathise with many elements in it which most Europeans (and all Americans) would call lazy and unprogressive. But when all allowance has been made for these moral merits, of the simpler sort, I defy anybody with a sense of cultural comparison to tolerate the image of Europe of the Renaissance given up to Bashi-Bazouks and the wild Mongol mobs of the decline. But it is almost as bad if we consider only the vetoes of primitive Islam; and most of its virtues were vetoes. When all is said, to the eyes of Mediterranean men especially, there passed across their shining sea merely the shadow of a great Destroyer. What they heard was the voice of Azrael rather than Allah. Theirs was the vision that would have been the background of my dream; and lifted all its nobler figures, English, Spanish, or Scottish, into the altitudes of defiance and martyrdom. The dry wind that drove before it a dust of broken idols was threatening the poised statues of Angelo and Donatello, where they shine on the high places around the central sea; and the sand of the high deserts descended, like moving mountains of dust and thirst and death, on the deep culture of the sacred vines; and the songs and the deep laughter of the vineyards. And above all, those clouds that were closing round them were like the curtains of the harem, from whose corners look out the stony faces of the eunuchs; there spread like a vast shadow over shining courts and closing spaces the silence of the East, and all its dumb compromise with the coarseness of man. These things, above all, were closing in upon that high and thwarted romance of the perfect Knight and Lady, which men of the Christian blood can never attain and never abandon; but which these two alone, perhaps, might have attained and made one flesh.

Historians quarrel about whether the English under Elizabeth preferred the Prayer-Book or the Mass-Book. But surely nobody will quarrel about whether they preferred the Crescent or the Cross. The learned dispute about how England was divided into Catholics and Protestants. But nobody will dispute what England would have felt, when told that the whole world was now desperately divided into Christians and Mohammedans. In short, I think that under this influence England would have simply broadened her mind; even if it were only broadened to take in a big battle instead of a small battle. Of that broader battle, and our best chances in it, Don John of Austria was universally regarded as the incarnation and the uplifted sign. Not only the praise due to heroes, but the flattery inevitably paid to princes, would have carried that triumph before him wherever he went like a noise of trumpets. Everybody would have felt in him both the Renaissance and the Crusade; as those two things are warp and woof in the golden tapestries of Ariosto. Everybody would have felt both the rebirth of Europe and its all-but death. Nor need the praise have come merely from any common flatterers. All good Englishmen could have become good Europeans; I should express my meaning better if I said great Europeans. In all that crowd, perhaps, only Shakespeare could not have been greater. And yet I am not so sure; for he might certainly have been gayer. Whatever his politics were (and I suspect they were much like those of his friend the Catholic Southampton) there is no doubt that his tragedies are eternally twisted and tortured with something like an obsession about usurpation and slain kings and stolen crowns; and all the insecurity of royal and every other right. Nobody knows how his heart, if not his mind, might have expanded in that truly "glorious summer" of a sovereignty which satisfied his sixteenth-century hunger for a heroic and high-hearted sovereign. He at least would not have been indifferent to the significance of the great triumph in the Mediterranean. Supporters of the extreme spiritual insularity have often quoted the great lines in which Shakespeare praised England, as something separate and cut-off by the sea. They rather tend to forget what he really praised her for.

> This nurse, this teeming womb of royal kings,
> Feared by their breed and famous by their birth,
> Renowned for their deeds as far from home,
> For Christian service and true chivalry,
> As is the sepulchre in stubborn Jewry
> Of the world's ransom, blessed Mary's Son.

I really think that the man who wrote those lines would have welcomed the victor of Lepanto almost as warmly as he must have welcomed a Scotch Calvinist who was frightened of a drawn dirk.

About Mary I imagine there would have been no difficulty at all. Mary was the perfectly legitimate heir to the throne of England, which is more than can be said for Elizabeth. The general sense of loyalty to the legitimate sovereign, which was enormously strong in England, would have flowed towards her more freely than towards Elizabeth; because she was a more popular and approachable sort of person. She who had so often, and perhaps too often, kindled love even in the very house of hatred, might surely have been loved sufficiently in a happier household of love enthroned; as in the glowing palace of René of Provence. I see no difficulty about her popularity; but even her husband, whether he were called Consort or King, might surely, to say the least of it, have been as popular as any other king-consort. I will not say he would be more popular than William of Orange; for he could not be less. But the English can be polite to foreigners, even foreign consorts. Tennyson, as Poet Laureate, was struck by the resemblance between Prince Albert and an ideal knight of the Round Table. Ben Jonson, as Poet Laureate, would not have to stretch politeness quite so far, in order to compare Don John to an Arthurian knight. At least nobody could say he was a carpet-knight. But, what is much more important, Britain would have been in another and more real sense back in Arthurian times. It would be defending the whole tradition of Roman culture and Christian morals against heathens and barbarians from the ends of the earth. If that had been fully realised, do you think anyone would have gone about asking whether a good Calvinist ought to be a Supralapsarian or a Sublapsarian? It would no longer be a provincial question of whether some Puritan trooper had knocked the nose off a stone saint in Salisbury Cathedral; it would be a question of whether some dervish out of the desert should dance among the shattered fragments of the Moses of Michelangelo. All normal Christians, if they had understood the peril, would have closed up in defence of Christendom. And England would have got glory in the battle, as she did when that ship with crimson sails carried the English leopards to the storming of Acre. It might, I fear, have meant a certain amount of hostility to France: the rival of the Spanish-Austrian combination; though even here there are reconciling influences and Mary's sympathies would always have been with the country of her youth and her most famous poem. But, anyhow, it would not have been like the hostility to France, or rather blind hatred of France, which we did inherit from the victory of the Whigs. It would have been more like the medieval wars with the French, waged by men who were half French themselves. The English conquests in France were a sort of eddy and backwash of the original French conquest in England; the whole business was almost a civil war. For there was more internationalism in medieval war than there is in modern peace. The same was true of the actual wars which did break out between France and Spain; they did not break the inner unity of the Latin culture. Louis the Fourteenth was guilty of a slight exaggeration in saying that the mountains called the Pyrenees have entirely disappeared from the landscape. Many careful tourists have verified their existence and reported the royal error. But there was this truth in it; that the Pyrenees were in every sense a natural division. The Straits of Dover soon became a very unnatural division. They became a spiritual abyss, not between different patron saints but between different gods; perhaps between different universes. The men who fought at Crecy and Agincourt had the same religion—to disregard. But the men who fought at Blenheim and at Waterloo had this entirely novel feature—that the English had an equal hatred for French religion and for French irreligion. They could not understand the ideals of either side in the great civil war of all civilisation. The limitation was really rather like the Straits of Dover, being both narrow and bleak and dangerous enough to be decisive; bitter as the sea and aptly symbolised by sea-sickness. Perhaps, after all, there was a point in the tale told in our nursery histories—that it was the last Catholic queen who felt the loss of the last French possession, and had "Calais" written on her heart. With her died, perhaps, the last of that spirit which had somewhere in its depths a spiritual Channel Tunnel. But this linking up of Europe in the Renaissance would have made easier and not harder the linking up of Europe in the Revolution; in the sense of the general Reform that was really rational and necessary in the eighteenth century. It would have been larger and clearer in its tests and ideals, if it had *not* been anticipated by a mere triumph of the richest aristocrats over the English crown. If England had not become entirely a country of squires, it might have become, like Spain, a country of peasants; or at any rate remained a country of yeomen. It might have stood the siege of commercial exploitation and commercial decline, of mere employment followed by mere unemployment. It might have learned the meaning of equality as well as liberty. I know at least one Englishman who wishes today that he were as hopeful about the immediate future of England as about the immediate future of Spain. But in my vision they might have learned from each other and produced, among other things, one prodigious consequence; America would be a very different place.

There was a moment when all Christendom might have clustered together and crystallised anew, under the chemistry of the new culture; and yet have remained a Christendom that was entirely Christian. There was a moment when Humanism had the road straight before it; but, what is even more important, the road also straight behind it. It might have been a real progress, not losing anything of what was good in the past. The significance of two people like Mary

Stuart and Don John of Austria is that in them Religion and the Renaissance had not quarrelled; and they kept the faith of their fathers while full of the idea of handing on new conquests and discoveries to their sons. They drew their deep instincts from medieval chivalry without refusing to feed their intellects on the sixteenth-century learning; and there was a moment when this spirit might have pervaded the whole world and the whole Church. There was a moment when religion could have digested Plato as it had once digested Aristotle. For that matter, it might have digested all that is soundest in Rabelais and Montaigne and many others; it might have condemned some things in these thinkers; as it did in Aristotle. Only the shock of the new discoveries could have been absorbed (to a great extent indeed it was absorbed) by the central Christian tradition. What darkened that dawn was the dust and smoke from the struggles of the dogmatising sectaries in Scotland, in Holland, and eventually in England. But for that, on the Continent, the heresy of Jansenism had never so much overshadowed the splendour of the Counter-Reformation. And England would have gone the way of Shakespeare rather than the way of Milton; which latter degenerated rapidly into the way of Muggleton.

There is perhaps, therefore, something more than a fancy, certainly something more than an accident, in this connection between the two romantic figures and the great turning-point of history. They might really have turned it to the right rather than the left; or at least prevented it from turning too far to the left. The point about Don John of Austria is that, like Bayard and a few others in that transition, he was unmistakably the original medieval knight, with the wider accomplishments and ambitions of the Renaissance added to him. But if we look at some of his contemporaries, as for instance, at Cecil, we see an entirely new type, in which there is no such combination or tradition. A man like Cecil is not chivalrous, does not want to be chivalrous, and (what is most important of all) does not pretend to be chivalrous. Of course there was sham chivalry, as there is a sham of everything; and mean and treacherous medieval men made a false parade of it with pageants and heraldry. But a mean man like Cecil did not make any parade of it, or any pretence of it. So far as he knew or cared, it had gone clean out of the world. Yet in fact it had not gone; and a great rally of it among his foes would still have commanded the natural loyalty of Europeans. That is what makes this story so strange; that the forces were there for the deliverance. The Romance of the North could really have replied to the Romance of the South, the rose crying to the laurel; and she who had changed songs with Ronsard, and he who had fought side by side with Cervantes, might truly have met by the very tide and current of their time. It was as if a great wind had turned northward, bearing a gallant ship; and far away in the North a lady opened her lattice upon the sea.

It never happened. It was too natural to happen. I had almost said it was too inevitable to happen. Anyhow, there was nothing natural, let alone inevitable, about what did happen. Now and again Shakespeare, with a horror almost bordering on hysteria, will thrust into the limelight some clown or idiot, to suggest, against the black curtain of tragedy, this incongruity and inconsequence in the things that really do happen. The dark curtains open and there comes forth something; certainly not the Lion of Lepanto clad in gold, nor the Heart of Holyrood, the queen of the poets, who called up the songs of Ronsard and Chastelard; but something quite different and doubtless a sort of comic relief: Jacobus Rex, the grotesque king; clumsy, querulous, padded like an armchair; pedantic; perverted. He had been brought up carefully by the elders of the True Kirk, and he did them credit;

piously explaining that he could not bring himself to save his mother's life because of the superstition to which she was attached. He was a good Puritan; a typical Prohibitionist; intolerant of tobacco; more tolerant of torture and murder and things yet more unnatural. For though he shook with terror at the very shape of the shining sword, he had no difficulty about consigning Fawkes to the rack, and when death had merely been attained by the art of poisoning, he was ready with a pardon, as he cowered under the threats of Carr. What things lay behind those threats and that pardon there is here, I am glad to say, no need to inquire; but the stink of that court, as it reaches us through the purlieus of the Overbury Murder, is such as to make us turn for fresh air. I will not say to the ideal loves of Mary and Don John of Austria, which I have merely imagined, but to the very worst version of the bloody loves of Mary and Bothwell which their most furious enemies have denounced. Compared with all that, loving Bothwell would be as innocent as plucking a rose, and killing Darnley as natural as pulling up a weed.

And so, after that one wild glimpse of the possibility of the impossible, we sink back at the best into a series of third-rate things. Charles the First was better, a man sad and proud, but good so far as a man can be good without being good-humoured. Charles the Second was good-humoured without being good; but the worst of him was that his life was a long surrender; James the Second had his grandfather's virtues, so far as they went, and was therefore betrayed and broken. Then came William the Dutchman, with whom there again enters the savour of something sinister and alien. I would not suggest that such Calvinists were Antinomian Calvinists; but there is something strange in the thought that twice, in that time, there entered with that unnatural logic the rumour and savour of unnatural desire. But by the time we come to Anne and the first featureless George, it is no longer the King that counts. Merchant princes have superseded all other princes; England is committed to mere commerce and the capitalist development; and we see successively established the National Debt, the Bank of England, Wood's Halfpence, the South Sea Bubble, and all the typical institutions of Business Government. I will not discuss here whether the modern sequel, with its cosmopolitan trusts, its complicated and practically secret financial control, its march of machinery and its effacement of private property and personal liberty, be on the whole good or bad. I will only express an intuition that, even if it is very good, something else might have been better. I need not deny that in certain respects the world has progressed in order and philanthropy; I need only state my suspicion that the world might have progressed much quicker. And I think that the northern countries, especially, *would* have progressed much quicker, if the philanthropy had been from the first guided by a larger philosophy, like that of Bellarmine and More; if it had drawn directly from the Renaissance and not been deflected and delayed by the sulky sectarianism of the seventeenth century. But in any case the great moral institutions of modern times, the Straddle, the Wheat Corner, the Merger, and the rest will not be affected by my little literary fancy; and I need feel no responsibility if I waste some hours of my inefficient existence in dreaming of the things that might have been (which the determinists will tell me could never have been) and in weaving this faded chaplet for the prince of heroes and the queen of hearts.

Perhaps there are things that are too great to happen, and too big to pass through the narrow doors of birth. For this world is too small for the soul of man; and, since the end of Eden, the very sky is not large enough for lovers.

Originally from *London Mercury*, February 1931
Reprinted in *The Common Man*

# BIBLIOGRAPHY

"The Battle of Lepanto", *Atlantic Monthly*. December 1857, pp. 138–48.

Beeching, Jack. *The Galleys at Lepanto*. New York: Charles Scribner's Sons, 1983.

Belloc, Hilaire. *The Great Heresies*. London: Sheed and Ward, 1938.

———. *On the Place of Chesterton in English Letters*. London: Sheed and Ward, 1940.

Benedict XV. *Fausto Appetente Die*: Encyclical of Pope Benedict XV on St. Dominic. St. Peter's in Rome, June 29, 1921.

Cervantes, Miguel de. *The History of Don Quixote de la Mancha*. Chicago: The University of Chicago, 1952.

Chesterton, G. K. *The Collected Works of G. K. Chesterton*. San Francisco: Ignatius Press, 1986– . (References are indicated by "*CW*" followed by volume and page.)

———. *The Common Man*. New York: Sheed and Ward, 1950.

———. *A Handful of Authors: Essays on Books and Writers*. London: Sheed and Ward, 1953.

———. *Lunacy and Letters*. London: Sheed and Ward, 1958.

———. *The Penguin Complete Father Brown*. New York: Penguin Books USA, 1981.

———. *The Poet and the Lunatics*. New York: Sheed and Ward, 1955.

———. *The Queen of Seven Swords*. London: Sheed and Ward, 1926.

Davies, Reginald Trevor. *The Golden Century of Spain 1501–1621*. London: Macmillan, 1937.

Goodwin, Jason. *The Lords of the Horizons: A History of the Ottoman Empire*. London: Vintage Random House, 1999.

Grimm, Harold J. *The Reformation Era. 1500–1650*, New York: Macmillan, 1954.

Guilmartin, John F., Jr. "The Galley in Combat". *MHQ: The Quarterly Journal of Military History* 9, no. 2 (Winter 1997): 20–21.

———. "Lepanto: The Battle that Saved Christendom?" Prepared for the *Centre d'Études d'Histoire de la Défense* conference *Autour de Lépante: Guerre et Géostratégie en Méditerranée au Tournant des XVIe et XVIIe Siecles,* Paris, October 22–24, 2001.

———. "The Tactics of the Battle of Lepanto Clarified: The Impact of Social, Economic, and Political Factors on Sixteenth Century Galley Warfare". *New Aspects of Naval*

*History: Selected Papers Presented at the Fourth Naval History Symposium, United States Naval Academy 25–26 October 1979.* Edited by Craig L. Symonds. Annapolis, Md.: The United States Naval Institute, 1981, pp. 41–65.

Hanson, Victor Davis. *Carnage and Culture: Landmark Battles in the Rise of Western Power.* New York: Doubleday, 2001.

Leckie, Robert . *Warfare.* New York: Harper and Row, 1970.

Leo XIII. *Augustissimae Virginis Mariae*: Encyclical of Pope Leo XIII on the Confraternity of the Holy Rosary. St. Peter's in Rome, September 12, 1897.

———. *Laetitiae Sanctae*: Encyclical of Pope Leo XIII Commending Devotion to the Rosary. St. Peter's in Rome, September 8, 1893.

Medcalf, Stephen. "The Achievement of G. K. Chesterton". In *G. K. Chesterton: A Centenary Appraisal* edited by John Sullivan. New York: Harper and Row, 1974.

Montross, Lynn. *War Through The Ages.* New York: Harper and Row, 1960.

O'Connell, Marvin R. *The Counter Reformation 1559–1610.* New York: Harper and Row, 1974.

O'Connor, John. *Father Brown on Chesterton.* 2nd ed. London: Frederick Muller, 1938.

Palmer, R. R., ed. *Historical Atlas of the World.* Chicago: Rand McNally, 1961.

Sodano, Angelo. "Homily at the Shrine of Our Lady of the Rosary of Pompei". Wednesday, May 8, 2002. Vatican archives, St. Peter's in Rome, 2003.

Thurston, Herbert J., S.J., and Donald Attwater, eds. *Butler's Lives of the Saints.* 4 vols. Allen, Tex.: Christian Classics, 1996.

Wahlig, Charles, "Our Lady of Guadalupe at the Decisive Moment in the Battle of Lepanto" in *A Handbook on Guadalupe.* New Bedford, Mass.: Franciscan Friars of the Immaculate, 1997.

Ward, Maisie. *Gilbert Keith Chesterton.* New York: Sheed and Ward, 1943.

————. *Return to Chesterton.* New York: Sheed and Ward, 1952.

# CONTRIBUTORS

**Dale Ahlquist** is president of the American Chesterton Society, publisher of *Gilbert Magazine*, author of *G. K. Chesterton: The Apostle of Common Sense*, editor of *The Gift of Wonder: The Many Sides of G. K. Chesterton*, and associate editor of *The Collected Works of G. K. Chesterton*. He is a graduate of Carleton College (B.A.) and Hamline University (M.A.). He lives near Minneapolis, Minnesota.

**William Cinfici** graduated Phi Beta Kappa from Gettysburg College, with a degree in history, and is a member of Phi Alpha Theta, the honorary history society. He has contributed essays for the *Italian American Perspective*, the newsletter of the Italian American Cultural Center. He lives in Reading, Pennsylvania.

**Peter Floriani** holds a B.S. and M.S. from Lehigh University and a Ph.D. in computer science from Rensselaer Polytechnic Institute, Troy, New York. His research was used to assist molecular biologists in the study of RNA sequences. He is the author of *The Faithful Home of the Three Stars*, the history of the Beta Theta Pi college social fraternity. He is also the creator of the "Amber Chesterton Collection", an electronic arrangement of the writings of G. K. Chesterton. He lives in Reading, Pennsylvania.

**Col. Melvin "Buzz" Kriesel** is a retired U.S. Army Special Forces officer. He is a graduate of West Point and has advanced degrees from the University of Minnesota and the

Army War College. He commanded Special Forces, intelligence, and PSYWAR units during a career that spanned forty years of military service. He now devotes his time to studying and writing about military history and the impact psychological factors have on warfare. He lives in Somerset, Wisconsin.

**Brandon S. Rogers** holds a B.S. in history from Central Michigan University and has studied Reformation history at Cambridge University in England. He works professionally in electronic communications and has assisted Dr. Floriani's efforts with the "Amber Chesterton Collection". He lives in Howell, Michigan.